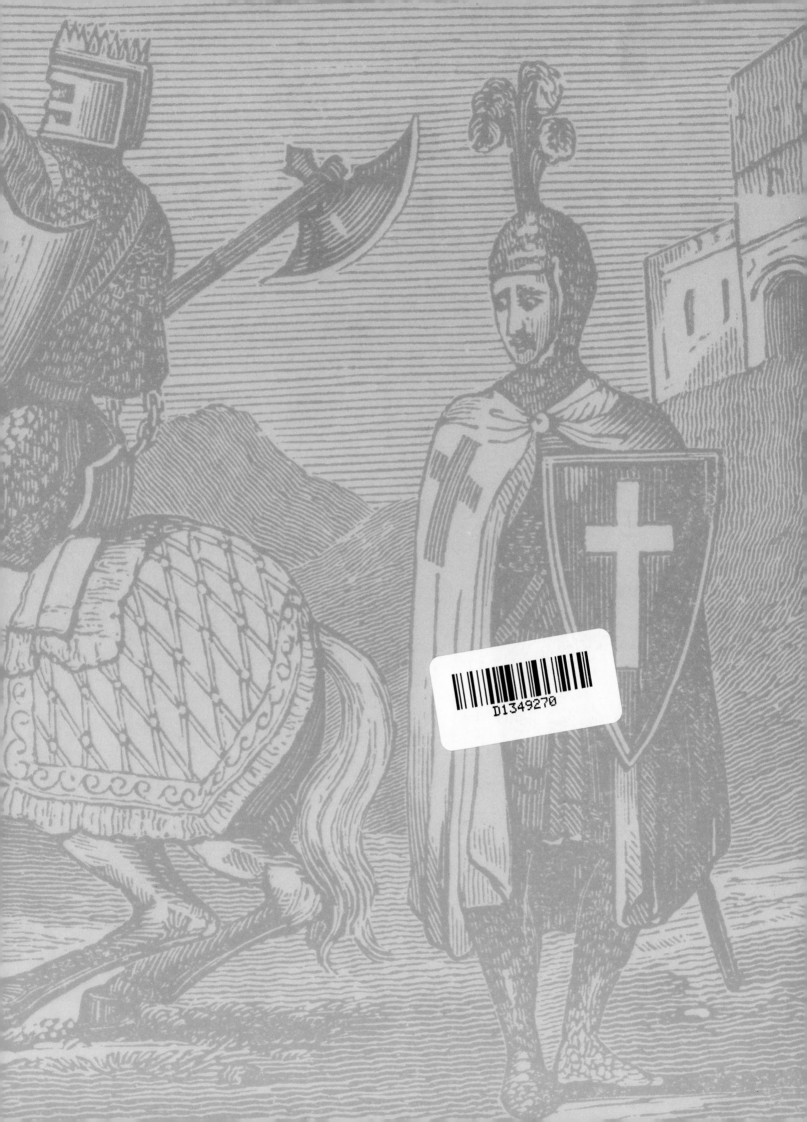

THE SECRET HISTORY OF THE
Knights Templar

THE SECRET HISTORY OF THE
Knights Templar

A COMPLETE ILLUSTRATED CHRONICLE OF THE RISE AND FALL OF ONE OF HISTORY'S
MOST SECRETIVE AND CONSPIRATORIAL BROTHERHOODS, FROM ITS ORIGINS AS A CHAMPION
OF CHRIST IN THE MIDDLE AGES TO ITS MYSTERIOUS LEGACY IN THE PRESENT DAY,
ILLUSTRATED WITH MORE THAN 200 FINE ART IMAGES

SUSIE HODGE

LORENZ BOOKS

This edition is published by Lorenz Books

Lorenz Books is an imprint of Anness Publishing Ltd
Hermes House, 88–89 Blackfriars Road, London SEI 8HA
tel. 020 7401 2077; fax 020 7633 9499
www.lorenzbooks.com; www.annesspublishing.com

Anness Publishing has a new picture agency outlet for images for
publishing, promotions or advertising. Please visit our website
www.practicalpictures.com for more information.

ETHICAL TRADING POLICY

At Anness Publishing we believe that business should be conducted in an
ethical and ecologically sustainable way, with respect for the environment
and a proper regard to the replacement of the natural resources we
employ. As a publisher, we use a lot of wood pulp to make high-quality
paper for print, and that wood commonly comes from spruce trees. We
are therefore currently growing more than 500,000 trees in two Scottish
forest plantations near Aberdeen – Berrymoss (130 hectares/320 acres)
and West Touxhill (125 hectares/305 acres). The forests we manage
contain twice the number of trees employed each year in paper-making
for our books.

Because of this ongoing ecological investment programme, you, as our
customer, can have the pleasure and reassurance of knowing that a tree is
being cultivated on your behalf to naturally replace the materials used to
make the book you are holding.

Our foresty programme is run in accordance with the UK Woodland
Assurance Scheme (UKWAS) and will be certified by the internationally
recognized Forest Stewardship Council (FSC). The FSC is a non-
government organization dedicated to promoting responsible
management of the world's forests. Certification ensures forests are
managed in an environmentally sustainable and socially responsible basis.
For further information about this scheme, go to
www.annesspublishing.com/trees.

© Anness Publishing Ltd 2006, 2008

UK agent: The Manning Partnership Ltd
sales@manning-partnership.co.uk

UK distributor: Grantham Book Services Ltd
orders@gbs.tbs-ltd.co.uk

North American agent/distributor:
www.nbnbooks.com

Australian agent/distributor: Pan Macmillan Australia customer.service@macmillan.com.au

New Zealand agent/distributor: David Bateman Ltd
tel. (09) 415 7664; fax (09) 415 8892

A CIP catalogue record for this book is available from the
British Library.

Designed and produced for Anness Publishing by
THE BRIDGEWATER BOOK COMPANY LTD.

Publisher Joanna Lorenz
Editorial Director Helen Sudell
Art Director Michael Whitehead
Production Controller Claire Rae

PICTURE ACKNOWLEDGEMENTS

Anness Publishing would like to thank the following for kindly supplying photographs for
this book: 1 Topfoto: 2 Picture Desk (PD): 3 Bridgeman Art Library: 4 PD: 5 bl PD, bc
Corbis, br Corbis: 6–7 PD: 8 b PD: 9 tl Topfoto, tr Corbis: 10 bl PD, br Bridgeman Art
Library: 11 tl PD, tr PD, br Bridgeman Art Library: 12–13 PD: 14 tl Corbis: 15 tr PD, br
Topfoto: 16 bl PD, br Bridgeman Art Library: 17 t PD, cr Tim Wallace-Murphy,
Bridgeman Art Library: 18 tl PD, tr PD: 19 tr PD, cr Tim Wallace-Murphy, bl PD: 20 tr
Bridgeman Art Library, bl PD: 21 tr Corbis, cr PD, cl PD: 22 tr PD, bl PD: 23 tr PD, bl
Mary Evans Picture library: 24 tl Corbis, br Corbis: 25 tl Tim Wallace-Murphy, br iStock
photography, bl PD: 26 tr Akg-images, bl PD: 27 t Akg-images, br iStock photography: 28 tr
Corbis, bl PD: 29 tr PD, br Corbis, cl Corbis: 30-31 PD: 32 tl Bridgeman Art Library, br
Mary Evans Picture library: 33 tl Topfoto, tr PD: 34 tr Corbis: 35 tl Corbis, cr iStock
photography: 36 bl PD: 37 tl Bridgeman Art Library, tr PD, bc PD: 38 tl Corbis, br Tim
Wallace-Murphy: 39 tl Corbis, br Alamy: 40 tr Tim Wallace-Murphy, bl Corbis: 41 tr iStock
photography, bc Bridgeman Art Library: 42 bl PD, br PD: 43 tl Corbis, cr PD: 44 tr Corbis,
bl PD: 45 br PD: 46 tl PD, br PD: 47 tl PD, cr PD: 48 tl Corbis: 49 tl PD, tr Corbis, br
PD: 50 cl Tim Wallace-Murphy: 51 tr Corbis, br PD: 52 tl Topfoto, br Corbis: 53 t Topfoto,
cr Mary Evans Picture library, br Corbis: 54–55 Corbis: 56 tl Corbis, tr Corbis: 57 tr PD, bl
Corbis: 58 br PD, bl Bridgeman Art Library: 59 t PD, cr Topfoto: 60 bl Corbis: 61 tl PD, tr
Corbis, br Bridgeman Art Library: 62 tr Corbis, bl PD: 63 tr PD, br Corbis: 64 tr PD, bl
Bridgeman Art Library: 65 tl Bridgeman Art Library, tr Corbis, cl PD: 66 tr Bridgeman Art
Library, bl PD: 67 t Corbis, br PD: 68 tr Topfoto, bl Corbis: 69 tr Temple Lodge photos, br
Corbis: 70–71 Topfoto: 72 tr PD, bl PD: 73 tl PD, tr PD: 74 tr PD, bl PD: 75 tr Tim
Wallace-Murphy, bl Tim Wallace-Murphy: 76 tr iStock photography: 77 tl PD, br PD: 78 tr
Bridgeman Art Library, bl iStock photography: 79 tr Alamy, br PD: 80 tl iStock
photography, br PD: 81 t Corbis, cr Corbis, br Tim Wallace-Murphy: 82 tr PD, bl PD: 83 tl
Corbis, br PD: 84 tr PD, bl iStock photography: 85 tr PD, bl PD: 86 t PD, bl PD: 87 tr
iStock photography, cr PD: 88 br iStock photography, bl PD: 89 tl Corbis, tr Tim Wallace-
Murphy, br PD: 90 tl Bridgeman Art Library, br PD: 91 t iStock photography, cr iStock
photography, br Akg-images: 92 tc Corbis, bl Bridgeman Art Library: 93 tc iStock
photography, tr Tim Wallace-Murphy, bl Corbis: 94 tr Corbis, bl Akg-images: 95 bc Mary
Evans picture library: 96 tr Tim Wallace-Murphy, bl PD.

Every effort has been made to obtain permission to reproduce copyright material, but there
may be cases where we have been unable to trace a copyright holder. The publisher will be
happy to correct any omissions in future printings.

Images are listed in clockwise order from the top (t = top, c = centre, b = bottom, r = right,
l = left, tr = top right, etc.)

Frontispiece: A twentieth-century illuminated manuscript from Languedoc, showing the
capture of Montségur Castle, France, where over 200 Cathars were burned alive during the
thirteenth-century Albigensian Crusade. In March 1244, 10,000 French Catholic troops set
fire to the castle, turning the Cathar defenders into a human bonfire.

CONTENTS

PART ONE

INTRODUCTION

The Knights Templar started life as the Order of the Poor Knights of the Temple of Solomon, or the Order of the Temple. Founded by the French nobleman Hugues de Payens in c 1118 in Jerusalem, this was the first military-religious order in Western Christendom. Men entered the order by taking vows and they lived according to a Rule, which included celebrating Mass. However, instead of devoting themselves to meditation and God's work, as in the Benedictine and Cistercian orders, they operated as a military organization in the service of God and his church. Their initial purpose was to protect Christian pilgrims in the Holy Land from attack. Over time, the Order became powerful and respected. Yet, in less than 200 years after it had formed, it fell spectacularly from grace.

RIGHT The Templars were both monks and soldiers, making them, in effect, some of the earliest "warrior monks" in the Western world. Members of the Order played a key part in many battles of the Crusades.

THE LEGEND

THE MYSTERIES SURROUNDING THE TEMPLARS HAVE BEEN CONFUSING AND CONFLICTING TO SAY THE LEAST. IN THE SEVEN CENTURIES SINCE THE FALL OF THE TEMPLARS, SPECULATION HAS BEEN RIFE. WHO WERE THEY? WHY DID THEY FORM AND WHY DID THE ORDER FALL SO DRAMATICALLY? WHAT WAS THE TRUTH ABOUT THEIR AIMS, IDEALS AND ACTIVITIES? WERE THEY HEROIC SOLDIER-MONKS WHO GUARDED INNOCENT PILGRIMS — ARCHETYPAL CRUSADERS AND DEFENDERS OF THE HOLY LAND WHO FOUGHT ALONGSIDE RICHARD THE LIONHEART, OR HERETICS AND WORSHIPPERS OF STRANGE BEINGS? PERHAPS MOST MYSTERIOUS OF ALL — WERE THEY IN POSSESSION OF SECRET TREASURES, AND WAS ONE OF THESE TREASURES THE HOLY GRAIL?

BELOW Twelfth-century fresco of crusading Knights Templar setting off to the Battle of Boquée, to fight the Infidels of Nour ed-Din.

Along with romantic notions, far more sinister legends have evolved around the Templars, including stories of necromancy (predicting the future by calling up spirits) and blasphemy.

At the beginning of the fourteenth century, the Templars were put on trial and these accusations were used against them. Even now, some question whether there was any truth in this.

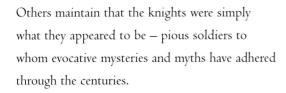

Others maintain that the knights were simply what they appeared to be – pious soldiers to whom evocative mysteries and myths have adhered through the centuries.

THE ELUSIVE TRUTH

One of the main reasons that there is so much controversy and contradiction over what the Templars were really like and what they knew is because a great deal of documentation was destroyed after their demise. This lack of solid evidence has given rise to accounts that have been inconsistent and contradictory at times and credible and convincing at others. Furthermore, there is much debate over material that has been produced far more recently. Nevertheless, certain documentation and archaeological evidence can be analysed and some of the elusive history pieced together.

Having been passed down and accepted as authentic, many of the "facts" about the Templars are probably assumptions. The first source of information on the Order is generally accepted as

being the historical documents of Guillaume de Tyre (died c 1186), but even these have been brought into question. Not much is known about de Tyre's sources and certain verifiable dates are inaccurate. As he began writing when the Templars had been in existence for about 50 years, it has been questioned whether he was recording facts, drawing on accepted opinion, or simply relating what the Templars had told him. Michael the Syrian, the Patriarch (Catholic Archbishop) of Antioch (died 1199) and Walter Map, Archdeacon of Oxford (died between 1208 and 1210), also wrote about the Templars, but they too were writing long after the Order began. Nevertheless, these accounts remain valuable sources of fundamental information about the Order.

ABOVE Knight from the Second Crusade praying. The Second Crusade to be launched from Europe was called in 1145 in response to the fall of the County of Edessa. Organized by the Pope and led by Kings, European Christians truly believed that they were doing God's work as they fought for land in Outremer.

ABOVE LEFT Jacques de Molay, last Grand Master of the Knights Templar. In the two centuries of their known existence, the Knights served under 23 Grand Masters. De Molay was the last and probably the best known Templar besides the founder of the Order, Hugues de Payens.

THE FOUNDING

THE KNIGHTS TEMPLAR FORMED AFTER THE FIRST CRUSADE, WHICH ENDED IN 1099. THEY WERE A MONASTIC MILITARY ORDER CREATED FROM A GROUP OF NINE KNIGHTS. JUST BEFORE 1118, THESE HUMBLE KNIGHTS CAME TOGETHER WITH THE AIM OF PROTECTING PILGRIMS TRAVELLING THROUGH THE HOLY LAND. SINCE THE FIRST CRUSADE 20 YEARS EARLIER, JERUSALEM WAS IN CHRISTIAN HANDS AND WAS THE PRINCIPAL DESTINATION FOR PILGRIMS FROM EUROPE. UNAWARE OF THE DANGERS THAT THEY MIGHT ENCOUNTER ON THE WAY, PILGRIMS FLOCKED TO THE HOLY LAND. HOWEVER, CHRISTIANS WERE AT A SEVERE NUMERICAL AND LOGISTICAL DISADVANTAGE IN THE EAST, AND THE ROADS AND HIGHWAYS AROUND JERUSALEM WERE NOTORIOUS FOR THE BANDS OF ROBBERS THAT CONGREGATED THERE, PREYING ON INNOCENT PILGRIMS PASSING THROUGH THE AREA.

BELOW Godfroi de Bouillon (1061–1100), French Crusader elected King of Jerusalem in 1099. He preferred the title "Defender of the Holy Sepulchre".

The knights had no money of their own, no uniform – their clothes were donated – and they were constantly short of both new recruits and equipment. They relied on the benevolence and alms of the King of Jerusalem, Baldwin II, whose cousin Godfroi de Bouillon had captured the Holy City 19 years before. When Godfroi died in 1100, his younger brother Baldwin became the Defender of the Holy Sepulchre and King of Jerusalem, and from 1118 their cousin Baldwin II took the throne. He showed his respect for the Templars by granting them accommodation in a wing of his palace, with large enough quarters to house them and their horses comfortably. This palace and the Templars' quarters were on the site of the ancient Temple of Solomon, and it was from here that they derived their name.

ABOVE The al-Aqsa Mosque on the Temple Mount in Jerusalem, known as the Temple of Solomon by the Crusaders. It was the Templars' head-quarters until 1187, and it is from here that the Knights Templar derived their name.

INFLUENCE

The Templars were unusual in that they were brothers of a religious order, and also soldiers. They united the knightly and religious roles that were at the heart of medieval society in the early twelfth century. They played a key part in many battles of the Crusades, yet they devised numerous financial innovations that could be considered the basis of modern banking. Credibility and validation for the Templars came when Bernard of Clairvaux, a zealous and charismatic Cistercian monk with important family connections, became their champion. In 1130, Bernard walked miles to convince countless influential people to accept the unpopular Innocent II as Pope. After Innocent's inauguration, Bernard became the most influential monk of his time.

Bernard was related to and friends with some of the first Templars, and with Hugues, the Count of Champagne (not to be confused with Hugues de Payens). The Count was involved with the Templars' foundation and he gave Bernard some land in the valley of Wormwood. Here, Bernard founded an abbey, renaming the area Clairvaux,

Valley of Light. Bernard wrote the first Rules of the Templar Order in 1128, basing these on the Rule adopted by the Cistercians, of whom he had been a faithful member since the age of 23. In 1139, the Templars were officially declared to be a monastic order under the protection of the Church in Troyes. With Bernard's influence, Innocent II recognized them as being solely under the authority of the papacy. Bernard died in Clairvaux on 20 August 1153. The date became his feast day. He was canonized in 1174.

THE CISTERCIANS

Also known as the White Monks because their habits were made of un-dyed white wool, the Cistercians were an order founded by Robert of Molesme at Cîteaux, France, in 1098. They were a strict reformed branch of the Benedictines and were expanded by Bernard of Clairvaux. The Cistercians lived by agricultural labour and made several advances in medieval farming methods. They lived in remote areas and led simple, austere lives. Many of their abbeys were dedicated to St Mary.

ABOVE Bronze coin of Baldwin II, King of Jerusalem (1118–31) and benefactor of the Knights Templar, depicting him wearing chain mail and conical helmet.

PART TWO

THE ORDER
OF THE TEMPLE

 It is generally accepted that the Order of the Poor Knights of Christ and the Temple of Solomon was founded by Hugues de Payens and his eight companions in 1118 after the First Crusade, though the Order may have existed before this "official" starting date. De Payens was from the Champagne region. It is thought that he took his knight comrades to Baldwin's palace in Jerusalem to offer themselves as a monastic military order. Their declared objective was to keep the roads and highways safe, with special regard for the protection of pilgrims. The first nine knights were: Hugues de Payens, Geoffrey de St Omer, Payen de Montdidier, Archambaud de St Agnan, André de Montbard, Geoffrey Bisol, and two knights recorded as Rossal and Gondamer. The ninth member is unknown, although some suggest that it was Hugues, the Count of Champagne.

RIGHT Meeting of the Knights Templar in Paris, organized by Robert the Burgundian, in the presence of Louis VII of France and Pope Eugene III on 22 April 1147.

THE FIRST CRUSADE

THE FIRST CRUSADE WAS LAUNCHED BY POPE URBAN II TO REGAIN CONTROL OF JERUSALEM AND ALLOW PILGRIMS ACCESS TO CHRISTIAN HOLY SITES. THE MUSLIMS HAD CAPTURED THE CITY IN 1076, AND THE BYZANTINE EMPEROR, ALEXIUS I, WAS CONCERNED THAT HIS COUNTRY MIGHT ALSO FALL TO THE MUSLIMS, AS THEY WERE TAKING CONTROL OF LARGE PARTS OF EASTERN EUROPE. ALEXIUS APPEALED TO THE POPE WHO, ON 27 NOVEMBER 1095, ADDRESSED A HUGE CROWD AT CLERMONT, FRANCE: "CHRISTIANS, HASTEN TO HELP YOUR BROTHERS IN THE EAST, FOR THEY ARE BEING ATTACKED. ARM FOR THE RESCUE OF JERUSALEM UNDER YOUR CAPTAIN CHRIST. WEAR HIS CROSS AS YOUR BADGE. IF YOU ARE KILLED, YOUR SINS WILL BE PARDONED".[1]

People of all ages, abilities and backgrounds flocked to fight; more than anyone had expected. To begin with, most were not knights but poor men, women and children. Among their numbers were those who believed they would find riches in the East, fervent Christians who wanted to reclaim Jerusalem, and those who believed that fighting for God would give them absolution. Others went because Crusaders did not pay tax.

PETER THE HERMIT

Urban II planned the departure of the Crusade for 15 August 1096, but before this an army of peasants set off on their own. Led by a charismatic monk from Amiens known as Peter the Hermit, some 100,000 men, women and children marched in the spring of 1096. Peter claimed he had a letter from God authorizing the Crusade. Bishops tried to restrain the old

ABOVE Peter the Hermit is thought to be one of the main instigators of the First Crusade. His speeches appealed not only to knights, but to labourers and peasants. It was these poor and untrained people who followed him readily to Constantinople, in what became known as "The People's Crusade".

RIGHT Map showing the routes of the unofficial and official Crusaders during the First Crusade.

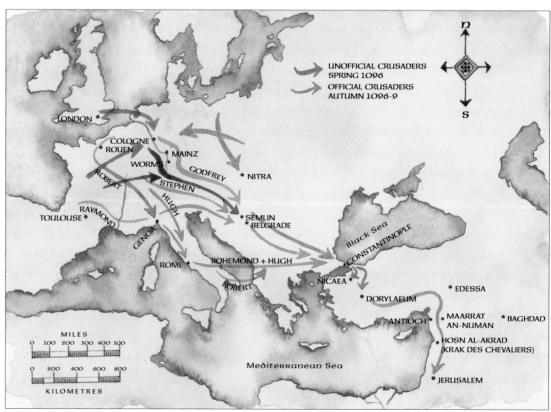

and sick from going, monks were forbidden to go, and husbands were not meant to go without their wives' consent, but many went anyway.

The People's Army, as it became called, got off to a bad start. On their way down the Danube, some looted Hungarian territory and were attacked by Hungarians and Bulgarians. About a quarter of them were killed. The remaining three-quarters continued into Constantinople along with other gathering armies. Alexius, not happy about the intrusion, helped them across the River Bosphorus. Once into Asia Minor they were all massacred by Turks, although Peter survived and later joined the main Crusaders.

THE REPERCUSSIONS

After an arduous and dangerous journey, the "official" Crusaders finally reached and overcame Jerusalem in the summer of 1099. The ultimate result of the First Crusade was the establishment of four Latin states or kingdoms in the Middle East: the County of Edessa, the Principality of Antioch, the County of Tripoli and the Kingdom of Jerusalem.

THE ENEMIES OF CHRIST?

The Islamic translations for the words "Franks" and "Crusaders" became terms of contempt in the Islamic world, as the Crusades were regarded as savage attacks by Christians.

In parts of France and Germany, Jews were perceived as just as much an enemy as Muslims

and many people wondered why they should travel thousands of miles to fight non-believers when there were already plenty closer to home. In the summer of 1096, a German army marched in the opposite direction of Jerusalem, believing that all Jews as well as Muslims were enemies of Christ and should be fought or converted to Christianity. No crusade had been declared against Jews, yet this created strong feelings of ill-will between both the Jews and the Christian Crusaders.

ABOVE Capture of Antioch during the First Crusade in 1098, from *Le Miroir Historial* by Vincent de Beauvais, fifteenth century.

BELOW A fourteenth-century illustration of two Knights Templar approaching the open gate to a city. On the battlements are three Saracen warriors.

HUMBLE BEGINNINGS

AFTER THE VICTORY OF THE FIRST CRUSADE, ONE OF THE LEADING CRUSADERS, GODFROI DE BOUILLON, WAS PROCLAIMED "DEFENDER OF THE HOLY SEPULCHRE". ALTHOUGH IT WAS SUGGESTED HE BE CALLED THE KING OF JERUSALEM HE REFUSED, SAYING ONLY JESUS HAD THE RIGHT TO BE CALLED THAT, BUT THE CHRISTIAN REALM OF JERUSALEM WAS ESTABLISHED. IN EUROPE, IT BECAME CALLED OUTREMER, WHICH TRANSLATES AS "THE LAND BEYOND THE SEAS".

BELOW The west side of the Dome of the Rock, Jerusalem, also known as the al-Aqsa Mosque, believed to be built on the site of Solomon's Temple. The Templars made part of this building their headquarters during the twelfth century.

Unexpectedly, Godfroi died in the autumn of 1100. His younger brother Baldwin assumed the title of the first King of Jerusalem. His realm extended from Beirut to the Red Sea. Various other principalities and kingdoms surrounded this land. Outremer was now, in effect, a collection of small kingdoms ruled by allied European nobles and modelled on the European feudal system.

PILGRIM SAFETY

Even when under Muslim control, Christian pilgrims had flocked to the Holy Land. Now that it was under Christian management, these pilgrims came in even greater numbers. Although all major cities of Outremer were in Christian hands, the roads were not safe. Once outside the city walls, the pilgrims were attacked by bands of robbers and assailants. By 1119, the situation was terrible. At Easter, 700 pilgrims were attacked by Saracens (a medieval term for Arabs) on the road to the River Jordan; 300 were killed and 60 were sold into slavery. By this time, Baldwin's successor, his cousin Baldwin II, had been on the throne of Jerusalem for a year. Baldwin approved of Hugues de Payens and Godfrey de St Omer's offer to

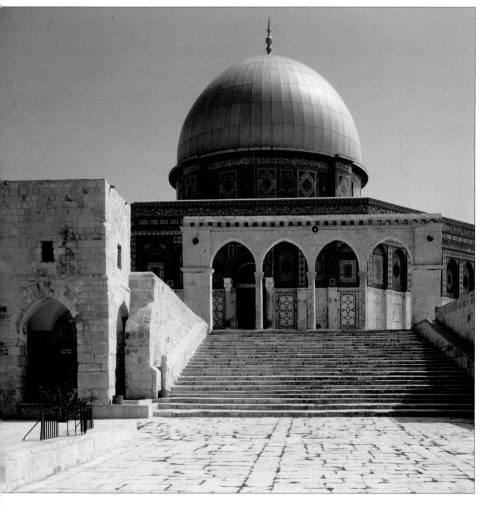

ABOVE This painting depicts the looting that took place in Jerusalem after its capture by the Christians during the First Crusade in 1099.

RIGHT At the Templar initiation ceremony, each knight took an oath of allegiance. Based on the Cistercian Rule, they also vowed oaths of poverty, chastity and obedience.

guard the pilgrims as they made their way to and from the holy sites. By also offering to live as monks following the Rule of St Augustine, they appeared to be more trustworthy and dependable than the usual sort of treasure-seekers who offered him their services.

Although this is the accepted view of the beginning of the Order, it has been suggested that the Templars might have formed at the request of Baldwin or Warmund, the Patriarch of Jerusalem, rather than on their own initiative. Simon, a monk of St Bertin, wrote in around 1135–7 that the first Templars were Crusaders who decided to remain in the Holy Land instead of returning to France.

CONTROVERSY OVER DATE

There is some controversy over the exact year of the Order's founding. The date that is documented by Guillaume de Tyre and by the Templars themselves is 1118. However, as twelfth-century France began each year on 25 March, what has been accepted as 1118 could conceivably have been 1119 in that calendar. Perhaps more curiously, in 1114 when the Count of Champagne was preparing for a journey to the Holy Land, he received a letter from the bishop of Chartres rebuking him for leaving his wife and vowing to join "La Milice du Christ" (Knights of Christ). This is the name by which the Templars were originally known (and the name that Bernard of Clairvaux called them).

If the Count of Champagne was going to join the Templars, they must have already formed in 1114. If so, the date of 1118 or 1119 may simply be the year they formed officially. Alternatively, the bishop could have been referring to a small group of Christians already in Outremer who were attempting to protect the holy sites. Other knights did group together to defend churches, monasteries and holy places against robbers, not all seeking formal religious recognition. It is curious that none of the chroniclers we know about refer to the beginning of the Order at all.

ABOVE The Templar seal, showing two knights on one horse, symbolizing the initial poverty of the Order; they could only afford one horse between every two men.

LEFT The Church of the Holy Sepulchre, Jerusalem. The church is venerated by many Christians as being built on the Hill of Calvary, where Jesus was crucified, according to the New Testament.

THE FIRST TEMPLE

IN AROUND 950BC, KING SOLOMON BUILT A TEMPLE IN JERUSALEM ON A SITE CHOSEN BY HIS FATHER, KING DAVID, WHO RECOGNIZED IT AS THE SPOT WHERE ABRAHAM HAD PREPARED TO SACRIFICE HIS SON ISAAC (OR ISHMAEL). THE SITE HAS BEEN KNOWN EVER SINCE AS THE TEMPLE MOUNT. AS ABRAHAM RAISED THE KNIFE TO KILL HIS ONLY CHILD, GOD ORDERED HIM TO STOP. HE TOLD ABRAHAM THAT FOR PROVING HIS LOVE, BLESSINGS WOULD BE HEAPED ON HIM AND HIS DESCENDANTS, THE JEWS.

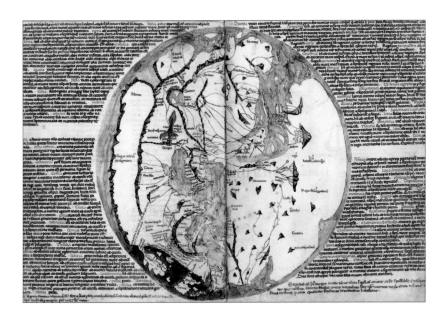

ABOVE Marino Sanudo the Elder (*c.*1206–1338) was a Venetian statesman and geographer. His work *Secreta fidelium crucis* ("Secrets of the Faithful of the Cross") was begun in March 1306 and was given to Pope Clement V in 1307 as a manual for Crusaders wanting to recapture the Holy Land.

ABOVE RIGHT King Solomon overseeing the construction of his Temple in Jerusalem, around 950BC. The construction of the First Temple was a monumental task carried out by Phoenician craftsmen. Building began in the fourth year of Solomon's reign and took seven years.

According to Jewish scripture, when Moses led the Jewish people out of Egypt and into the desert, God conveyed the Ten Commandments to him on Mount Sinai. The commandments were engraved on two stone tablets and later, to protect them, the Jews constructed a wooden box that they called the Ark of the Covenant. In around 623BC, King Josiah ordered: "Put the Holy Ark in the house which Solomon the son of David king of Israel did build".

Solomon's Temple became a place of pilgrimage and devotion, but in 586BC King Nebuchadnezzar of the Chaldeans ordered its destruction and had the Jews taken into slavery. In 515BC, Cyrus, the king of the Persians took power and allowed the Jews to return and rebuild their temple. By 167BC, the Jewish people were once more threatened by enemies and placed themselves under the protection of Rome.

The Romans took control, and in AD70 the Jews revolted but were crushed by the Romans, and the Temple was destroyed for a second time. In AD312 Emperor Constantine converted to Christianity and had churches built throughout Jerusalem. In AD638 the city fell into Muslim hands and the caliph Abd al-Malik built a major Islamic shrine, the Dome of the Rock, on the site of Solomon's temple, as it was also the site of the Prophet Mohammed's ascension to Heaven.

It became known as the al-Aqsa mosque and by 1118, King Baldwin II had converted it into his large palace.

POOR SOLDIERS OF JESUS CHRIST

On Christmas Day 1119, Hugues and Godfrey swore vows of poverty, chastity and obedience before Baldwin and Warmund the Patriarch of Jerusalem, in the Church of the Holy Sepulchre. Baldwin allowed the nine knights to set up quarters in one wing of the palace. As it was built over the ruins of Solomon's Temple, the knights created their name, the Poor Knights of the Temple of Solomon or the Poor Fellow-Soldiers of Jesus Christ and the Temple of Solomon, or the Knights of the Temple of Solomon. They often referred to themselves as the Knights of the Temple.

The knights used the mosque as their headquarters for 68 years and designed other Templar buildings in Europe after the architecture on Temple Mount. Templar seals were also often adorned with dome shapes.

Along with many grateful pilgrims, Baldwin and his nobles gave the Templars money – enough for their food and clothing. As new recruits joined the Order, they donated all their worldly possessions, and so the Templars survived.

ABOVE Painting by Tiepolo (1696–1770) of *The Sacrifice of Isaac*, which shows Abraham being stopped by divine light from an angel as he raises the knife to slay his son.

ABOVE The Templar seal was used to show documents' authenticity. This is the back view of the traditional Templars' seal and depicts the Dome of the Rock.

LEFT *Moses opening the Red Sea* by Colin de Coter (c.1455–1540), shows Moses leading the Jewish people out of Egypt and into the desert.

> ### THE CHURCH OF THE HOLY SEPULCHRE
>
> This church is built on the ground revered by Christians as Golgotha, the Hill of Calvary, where the New Testament states that Jesus was crucified. It is also said to contain the sepulchre where Jesus was reportedly buried. The church has been an important destination for Christian pilgrims since the fourth century. Today, it serves as the headquarters of the Orthodox Patriarch of Jerusalem and the Catholic Archpriest of the Basilica of the Holy Sepulchre.

THE NEW KNIGHTHOOD

FOR THE FIRST NINE YEARS, LITTLE IS KNOWN ABOUT THE ORDER'S ACTIVITIES. IT IS BELIEVED THAT THERE WAS NO INCREASE FROM THE FIRST NINE MEMBERS DURING THAT TIME AND HISTORIANS HAVE CONFLICTING THEORIES AS TO WHY THEY DID NOT EXPAND, CONSIDERING THE ONEROUS TASK OF PROTECTING HUNDREDS OF PILGRIMS ACROSS A BROAD AREA. SOME THEORIES SAY THAT NEW RECRUITS DID NOT COME FORWARD BECAUSE TEMPLAR LIFE WAS SO SEVERE, WHILE OTHERS CLAIM THAT THEY WERE BUSY ON SECRET BUSINESS SO DID NOT SEEK ANY NEW MEMBERS.

RIGHT A nineteenth-century engraving of an armed Templar in combat on his rearing horse, both in battle dress.

BELOW Interior view of Clairvaux Abbey, built in 1115 for the Cistercian monks who were led by Bernard, a staunch supporter of the Templars and who later became canonized. This stunning abbey was built in a valley on a tributary of the River Aube to the same plan as all Cistercian monasteries.

The Order that had been formed for a pious and military purpose was given Church recognition at the Council of Nablûs, in Palestine, in 1120, but this recognition did not extend officially outside Outremer. The Council of Nablûs was a council of lords who established the first written laws for the kingdom of Jerusalem after the First Crusade.

THE FIRST RECRUIT

Hugues, the Count of Champagne had first travelled to Outremer in 1104, remaining there for four years. In 1114 he returned again to join "La Milice du Christ". The Count came home to France in 1115 and donated land for Bernard's Abbey of Clairvaux. He returned once again to

the Holy Land in 1125, renounced his unfaithful wife, disinherited the son whom he believed was not his, and handed over the county of Champagne to his nephew, Theobald. He renounced his worldly wealth and joined the Templars. Hugues de Payens was one of the Count's vassals (men who promised military service and advice in return for a grant of land). By enlisting, the Count had to swear obedience to his own vassal, which created a curious anomaly. It is not clear whether or not he was directly involved in the original founding of the Order. It is viable that he was setting things up in the years he spent in the Holy Land, during 1104–8 and 1114–15. What is clear, however, is that he was involved with the Order from early on in its history.

BELOW Geoffrey Plantagenet, the son of Fulk (later Count) of Anjou. Like his father, he supported the Templars, as did his son, Henry II of England.

RIGHT Four Knights of the Temple of Solomon. By the twelfth century they were known throughout the Christian world for their courage and discipline.

A DIPLOMATIC MISSION

By the time he had formally joined, the Templars had clearly made a good impression on the King of Jerusalem. In 1127, Baldwin II sent them on an important diplomatic mission in Europe. He had no male heir, so he sent several nobles and nine Templars to France to persuade Fulk of Anjou to marry his daughter, Melisende, and so inherit the throne of Jerusalem after him. Hugues de Payens, as the Head of the Order, also had two further missions while in France. He had been instructed to recruit knights for a crusade against Damascus and to persuade the Western Church to officially recognize the Order.

The mission was extremely successful. Fulk agreed to return to Outremer and marry Melisende, a large army of knights were enlisted to fight in Damascus, and Hugues de Payens met Bernard of Clairvaux.

FULK OF ANJOU

At 38, Fulk of Anjou was a widower, a wealthy Crusader, and an experienced military commander, and so a valuable asset to Jerusalem. In 1131, he abdicated his county seat of Anjou to his son Geoffrey and took the throne of Jerusalem with Melisende on the death of Baldwin II. His friendship with and support of the Templars helped to establish their reputation and when he pledged to give them an annual income, other French nobles followed suit.

ABOVE Plan of the city of Damascus, Syria, from a sixteenth-century illustration. Damascus withstood a siege during the Second Crusade in 1148. In 1154, it was conquered by the famous Nur ad-Din of Aleppo, the great foe of the Crusaders. He made it his capital, and after his death, it was acquired by Saladin, the ruler of Egypt. Damascus steel gained a legendary reputation among the Crusaders.

THE COUNCIL OF TROYES

IN 1124–5, ST BERNARD OF CLAIRVAUX, APPRECIATING THE VOLATILE SITUATION FOR THE PILGRIMS IN OUTREMER, WROTE A LETTER TO POPE CALIXTUS II STATING THAT OUTREMER NEEDED KNIGHTS READY FOR ACTIVE SERVICE, NOT "SINGING AND WAILING MONKS". HIS UNDERSTANDING OF THE DIFFICULTIES PROBABLY CAME FROM HIS FRIENDSHIP WITH HUGUES DE CHAMPAGNE AND FROM HIS (YOUNGER) UNCLE, ANDRÉ DE MONTBARD, ONE OF THE FOUNDING MEMBERS OF THE TEMPLARS, WHO LATER BECAME ONE OF THE ORDER'S GRAND MASTERS.

RIGHT St Bernard, 1090–1153, teaching in a Dominican monastery, from a French manuscript of 1420–81. Bernard was a French abbot and the primary builder of the reforming Cistercian monastic order. He had converted the Rules of St Benedict for his foundation of the Cistercians. His charismatic speeches and teaching earned him recognition throughout Europe. He was the dominant figure in the Christian church and a champion of the Templars from about 1126 to 1153.

Hugues de Payens had written to Bernard to ask him to sponsor the Order, possibly through the suggestion of either André de Montbard or Hugues de Champagne. Bernard by now had considerable influence in the ecclesiastical world and his support was invaluable.

THE LATIN RULE

On 13 January 1128, an assembly of churchmen was convened by the Pope at Troyes, the capital city of Champagne. Bernard, and those Templars who were in Europe at the time, joined them.

The Council's purpose was to deal with Church matters, but as he had done previously, Bernard managed to use it for his own purposes. Hugues de Payens stood up to describe the origins of the

RIGHT Calixtus II, formerly Guy of Burgundy, Pope from 1119 to 1124, originated from Burgundy and was a member of the aristocracy. He was Pope during the early years of the Templars, but he had little to do with the small group of military monks in the Holy Land.

Templar Order and the rule by which they lived. He told of communal meals taken in silence, plain clothing, and vows taken of poverty, chastity and obedience.

After some discussion, the Council of Troyes, under Bernard's direction, drew up what became known as the Latin Rule of the Templars. It consisted of 73 clauses, to control every aspect of Templar life and it mirrored the rule of the Cistercians, with extra provision for when Templars were on active service. The Rule instructed on practically everything: how to

CLOTHING THE ORDER

The Rule stated that the Templars' habits or mantles would be of one colour: white, brown, or black, depending on their role within the Order. As with the Cistercians, the white habit signified purity and chastity. No fur or finery was allowed, even on their horses' bridles. Pride was punishable: "If any brother, out of a feeling of pride or arrogance wishes to have as his due a better and finer habit, let him be given the worst". One concession to the intensity of the heat in Palestine was the wearing of linen shirts from Easter to All Saints. All brethren had short hair with a monk's tonsure and all wore beards.

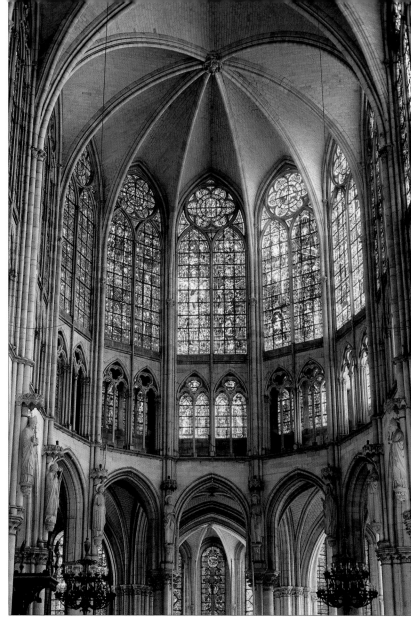

admit novices, the age of admittance, the length of time each man should serve, sanctions for bad behaviour and what offences should lead to exclusion from the Order. Brothers would eat two meals a day in silence, with meat eaten only three times a week. Unusually, married men were admitted, provided they had their wives' consent, but all physical relations were forbidden.

Brothers who sinned or infringed the Rule had to confess and do penance. A brother could be expelled from the Order for revealing its secrets, for buying or selling entrance to the Order, for killing a Christian, theft, desertion during battle, desertion to the Saracens or for sodomy. Lesser crimes included disobedience, striking another brother, having contact with a woman, charging into battle without permission and giving away the Order's possessions.

ABOVE The Cathedral of St Peter and St Paul in Troyes. Work began on this jewel of Gothic architecture in 1200 and continued until the middle of the sixteenth century. Troyes was the capital city of the region of Champagne, centre of the Cistercian Order and home of Hugues de Payens.

LEFT The Templars were recognizable by their distinctive white clothes adorned with a single red cross. Most unusual, perhaps, was their adherence to the regulation of wearing beards when cleanly shaven faces were more fashionable among Christians at that time.

THE HEAD OF THE ORDER

THE GRAND MASTER, BASED IN OUTREMER, WAS THE ABSOLUTE HEAD OF THE ORDER. ACCORDING TO THE RULE, TOTAL OBEDIENCE TO THE GRAND MASTER WAS REQUIRED AT ALL TIMES, SO STRICT INSTRUCTIONS WERE LAID DOWN FOR HIS SELECTION. A GROUP OF "THE WORTHY MEN OF THE HOUSE" VOTED TO SELECT ONE TO ACT AS A PRESIDING OFFICER. AFTER A NIGHT OF PRAYER, THIS OFFICER, TOGETHER WITH A DESIGNATED COMPANION, CHOSE TWO ADDITIONAL BROTHERS AND THE GROUP, IN TURN, ADDED TWO MORE UNTIL THEY NUMBERED 12, IN HONOUR OF THE 12 APOSTLES. THE ADDITION OF A CHAPLAIN TO TAKE THE PLACE OF CHRIST MADE THE ELECTORAL BODY 13 IN NUMBER. THE TEMPLARS ALWAYS TRIED TO INCLUDE EIGHT KNIGHTS, FOUR SERGEANTS AND ONE CHAPLAIN, AND TO INCLUDE AS MANY NATIONALITIES AS POSSIBLE. VOTING TOOK PLACE IN SECRET AND A MAJORITY DECISION WAS ESSENTIAL BEFORE THE NEW GRAND MASTER WAS ACCLAIMED BY THE BROTHERS.

RIGHT Portrait of Jacques de Molay, last Grand Master of the Knights Templar. De Molay had served as a Knight Templar from the age of about 20. He was elected Grand Master in 1293, when he was 49, and spent most of his time after that in Cyprus.

BELOW Portrait of Gualdim Pais, who became the fourth Master Templar of Portugal in 1157 (not the Grand Master in Jerusalem). He founded Tomar Castle in 1160 and supervised the building or restoration of several other frontier castles in Portugal. Pais died in Tomar in 1195.

The Grand Master answered only to the Pope, although he was governed by the Latin Rule, as were other members. Several Grand Masters became advisers to European monarchs. Each Grand Master was equipped with four horses, as opposed to the three that an ordinary Templar knight received. The Grand Master had his own sergeant and valet. The valet attended to the Master and carried his lance and shield.

Once elected, the Grand Master served for the rest of his life. He was also in charge of eight Templar provincial Masters who were in Aragon, Apulia, England, France, Poitiers, Hungary, Portugal and Scotland.

CHARITABLE BENEFACTORS

The founder and Grand Master of the Order, Hugues de Payens, had been given land in 1127 by Hugues de Champagne's nephew and successor, Theobald, Count of Blois. Soon after that, he was given more land and money and, in the summer of 1128, he was invited to England. There the Templars were given gifts of money and land and De Payens established their first preceptory (a monastic house) in London. He travelled on to Scotland and then Flanders, receiving further generous donations.

When Hugues returned to Outremer, he discovered that his Order was not universally welcomed. Many Christians believed in spiritual purity and condemned violence and bloodshed. The combination of monk and soldier was against their ideals. To justify the Templars' role, De Payens asked Bernard to compose a defence of the Order.

THE GRAND MASTERS

1118–1136 Hugues de Payens	1193–1200 Gilbert Erail
1136–1146 Robert de Craon	1201–1208 Philip de Plessiez
1146–1149 Everard des Barres	1209–1219 William de Chartres
1149–1153 Bernard de Tromelai	1219–1230 Pedro de Montaigu
1153–1156 André de Montbard	(....)–1244 Armond de Perigord
1156–1169 Bertrand de Blanchefort	1245–1247 Richard de Bures
	1247–1250 William de Sonnac
1169–1171 Philip de Milly	1250–1256 Reynald de Vichiers
1171–1179 Odo de St Amand	1256–1273 Thomas Berard
1179–1184 Arnold de Toroga	1273–1291 William de Beaujeu
1185–1189 Gerard de Ridefort	1291–1293 Tibauld de Gaudin
1191–1193 Robert de Sablé	1293–1314 Jacques de Molay

As their most powerful advocate and in accordance with De Payens' wishes, Bernard wrote a treatise, which he called *In Praise of the New Knighthood*. In it, he argued that the Templars' duty was to kill for Christ in order to rid the world of evil. He maintained that there was a difference between homicide, which was a sin, and malecide – the killing of evil – which was not a sin. As one of the most respected churchmen of the day, Bernard's words achieved their objective and so De Payens' position was strengthened once more. Land and buildings continued to be bestowed by donors who believed that in doing so, all their sins would be absolved.

LEFT St George was adopted as the patron saint of soldiers after he was said to have appeared to the Crusader army at the Battle of Antioch in 1098. When Richard I campaigned in Palestine between 1191 and 1192, he put the army under the protection of St George.

FAR LEFT Henry II (1133–89) was the first Plantagenet King of England and a big supporter of the Templar cause, as was his son Richard I (The Lionheart) who succeeded him on the throne. Henry – here, at his coronation – ruled England from 1154 until his death.

LEFT Kolossi castle on the island of Cyprus, originally constructed in the thirteenth century and subsequently rebuilt in its current form in the middle of the fifteenth century. It served as the Grand commandery of the Knights Templar and, after the fall of Acre in 1291, as the headquarters of the Order of St John of Jerusalem.

PAPAL APPROVAL

HUGUES DE PAYENS DIED ON OR AROUND 24 MAY 1136. HIS SUCCESSOR WAS ROBERT DE CRAON, KNOWN AS ROBERT THE BURGUNDIAN. HE PLANNED TO SECURE PAPAL APPROVAL AND IT TOOK HIM JUST THREE YEARS AS GRAND MASTER TO ACHIEVE THIS. ON 29 MARCH 1139, POPE INNOCENT II ISSUED A SPECIAL TYPE OF CHARTER CALLED A "BULL", ENTITLED THE *OMNE DATUM OPTIMUM*. THIS OFFICIALLY APPROVED THE POOR KNIGHTS OF THE ORDER OF THE TEMPLE OF SOLOMON, CONFIRMING THE RULE OF ORDER (THE LATIN RULE) AND ALL DONATIONS MADE TO THE TEMPLARS. THE POPE EXCUSED THE TEMPLARS FROM PAYING TITHES AND TAXES BUT ALLOWED THEM TO RECEIVE TITHES THEMSELVES, ON CONDITION THAT THESE WERE PRESENTED AS GIFTS AND FREELY GIVEN. THE TEMPLARS WERE ALSO GRANTED PERMISSION TO KEEP ALL SPOILS FROM THEIR MUSLIM CONQUESTS.

RIGHT The Coronation of Pope Clement V in 1305, who was Pope until his death in 1314. He is often remembered for his nepotism, avarice, weakness and cunning, and is often vilified as a willing collaborator in the suppression of the Order of the Templars.

BELOW Meeting of the Knights Templar in Paris on 22 April 1147. The ceremony took place in a chapter (a local branch of the brotherhood).

The *Omne Datum Optimum* was an unusual bull as it was so supportive of the Templars and it gave them so many privileges. It was followed by two more bulls, Celestine II's *Milites Templi* in 1144 and Eugenius III's *Militia Dei* in 1145, which both gave the Templars an even more extraordinary range of rights and privileges. Among other things, they were permitted to build their own churches, bury their dead in those church grounds and collect taxes on Templar properties once a year. These privileges were controversial among the many Europeans who struggled to pay their taxes – risking excommunication or eviction if they did not – while the Templars just grew richer.

FOR OR AGAINST

Over the 200 years between the First Crusade and the last Grand Master, there were 37 popes. Some were wholly supportive of and helpful to the Templars, while others, such as Clement V, who assisted their downfall, were opposed to them. Most were supportive though and through this papal support and protection, the Order of

the Poor Knights of the Temple of Solomon became firmly established at the centre of Christian life in the Holy Land. Their critics remained, but had no strength to oppose the knights now. In the 20 or so years since their founding, the Templars had risen higher than most other monastic orders and most other knights. As Innocent II had written in 1139: "...since your religious Order and your venerable institution is proclaimed throughout the whole world...you might be regarded especially as part of God's knighthood".[2]

THE RED CROSS

The early Templars wore a hauberk, or coat of mail, with a white surcoat and a padded leather jerkin underneath. Chain-mail hose covered their legs and they wore iron shoes and a conical helmet. They carried a shield, lance, Turkish mace

and three knives – a dagger, a bread knife and a pocket knife. It was not until 1147 that Pope Eugenius III (who had once been a monk at Clairvaux) granted them the right to wear the splayed red cross: a cross with spreading ends. It was sewn above the heart on the left side of the mantle. Knights wore a white mantle and sergeants wore brown, but after this date, all wore a red cross of the same size and in the same place.

ADDED POWER

Papal endorsement facilitated the Templars' quick rise. They used their growing recognition and papal privileges to their advantage, constructing numerous fortifications throughout the Holy Land, and were the best trained and most disciplined fighting units of their day. As more benefactors donated to them, their wealth, confidence and power increased.

ABOVE Twelfth-century mosaic (1140) showing an enthroned Christ with Mary and the saints Calixtus, Laurentius and Pope Innocent II holding a model of the church.

ABOVE The Templars had several shields and flags, and after 1147, all displayed their distinctive red cross *pattée* as the splayed cross was called.

FIGHTING THE INFIDEL

AT THE HEIGHT OF THEIR POWER, THE TEMPLARS WERE UNPARALLELED WARRIORS AND MONKS – THE
EMBODIMENT OF CHRISTIANITY'S CRUSADE AGAINST ISLAM. GIFTS OF LAND ACCEPTED ON THE ORDER'S
BEHALF WERE PUT TO IMMEDIATE USE TO PROTECT THE HOLY LAND AGAINST THE INFIDEL. ON HOLY
SITES WHERE PILGRIMS JOURNEYED, THE TEMPLARS BUILT FORTIFICATIONS AND SET UP PATROLS.

RIGHT The conquering
of Jerusalem during the
First Crusade, 1096–9.
For 39 days, Crusaders
besieged the Holy City,
until it finally fell on
15 July 1099 and they
replaced the crescent
with the cross on the
Dome of the Rock.

BELOW A Saracen army
on camels and horses
with standards flying
and musicians, from
an Arab manuscript.

At the Cisterna Rubea, midway between
Jerusalem and Jericho, the Templars built a castle,
a road station and a chapel. There was a Templar
tower closer to Jericho, a castle and priory on
the summit of Mount Quarantene, where Jesus
fasted for 40 days and was tempted by Satan,
and Jacob's Ford, a castle by the River Jordan,
where Jesus was baptized by John the Baptist.
Unfortunately, the Templars were still building
Jacob's Ford when Saladin's army attacked
in 1179. Without the castle's outer wall, the
Saracens gained access and destroyed both it
and the Templar garrison inside.

EXTENDED RESPONSIBILITIES

In the 1130s, Templars were given responsibility for
securing the mountainous frontier region north of
Antioch – the Amanus March. The castles that ran
through these mountains were maintained and
guarded by the Templars against the Cilician
Armenians and the Byzantine Greeks as well as
the Muslims. All castles here were fortified and the
Templars' reputation in upholding this area grew.

In Jerusalem, they were given the castle of Latrûn,
also known as Toron des Chevaliers, which was built
by Count Rodrigo Gonzalez of Toledo between
1137 and 1141, when he was in the Holy Land
fighting the Saracens. Gonzalez garrisoned and

Templars' coffers helped to alleviate worries
about lack of weapons, clothes or horses.

Within the Order, knights were in a minority,
with ranks of sergeants, squires and servants
making up the rest. The bulk of the Templar
army was made up of turcopoles, mounted
archers who were originally mainly Christians
of Arabic extraction, and so accustomed to the
Saracens' fighting methods. Turcopoles were more
lightly armoured than knights, with lances and
bows for greater mobility. Even Templar horses
were trained to kick and bite enemies. The
Templars followed the approach of Bernard of
Clairvaux, who declared that a small force under
the right conditions could defeat a much larger
enemy, and they became a major force in the fight
against Islam.

equipped the castle, then gave it to the Templars.
In 1149, after the Second Crusade, the Order was
given the fortress of Gaza. This had been built by
Baldwin III and his nobles as part of their plan to
surround the Muslim-held city of Ascalon, which
was on the coast ten miles to the north of Gaza.
Baldwin gave it to the Templars to use as a base
for raids against Ascalon and for protecting the
southern frontier of the kingdom of Jerusalem
against Egypt.

ELITE FIGHTING FORCE

By the 1130s, there were over 300 extremely
disciplined and well-armed Knights Templar.
The ever-increasing flow of money into the

ABOVE Twelfth-century
depiction of the battle
of La Bocquée, Syria,
between Hugues de
Lusignan, the Knight
Templar, and Emir Nour
ed-Din. This was part of
the Second Crusade.

LEFT Engraving after
a glass painting at the
Abbey of St Dennis,
France, portraying the
Battle of Ascalon, 1099,
between the Crusaders
and the Muslims.
Baldwin III seized
Ascalon in 1153.

BELOW Detail of
medieval crusading
knights from the stained
glass window at *Sainte
Chapelle* (French for
"The Holy Chapel"), a
Gothic chapel on the Île
de la Cité, in the heart of
Paris, France.

PART THREE

STRENGTHENING THE ORDER

 On admission to the Order, a man was required to sign over all his possessions, so it is hardly surprising that Templar assets multiplied so abundantly. Within a year of the Council of Troyes, the Order held substantial estates in France, England, Scotland, Flanders, Spain and Portugal. Although as individuals the Templars were bound to vows of poverty, the Order as a whole accumulated great wealth on an unparalleled scale. By the papal bulls, the Order was allowed to receive, but never to give. So by 1147, when Eugenius III had granted that they should wear the red cross, they owned vast tracts of territory. With this device emblazoned on their mantles, the now powerful knights accompanied King Louis VII of France on the Second Crusade. Here they established their reputation for military fervour and fearlessness.

RIGHT Louis VII, King of France 1120–80, leaving for the Second Crusade 1147–9.

THE ORDER'S HIERARCHY

THE GRAND MASTER WAS HEAD OF THE ENTIRE ORDER AND HE REMAINED IN THAT POSITION FOR LIFE. BECAUSE MOST GRAND MASTERS AND MOST OF THE ORIGINAL TEMPLARS WERE FRENCH, FRANCE WAS PARTICULARLY IMPORTANT TO THEM AND FRENCH KINGS OFTEN INFLUENCED THE CHOICE OF GRAND MASTER. THE SENESCHAL WAS THE GRAND MASTER'S DEPUTY AND WAS OCCASIONALLY PROMOTED TO THE POSITION OF GRAND MASTER, AS HAPPENED WITH ANDRÉ DE MONTBARD IN 1153. EACH COUNTRY ALSO HAD ITS OWN MASTER TEMPLAR, WHO WAS ANSWERABLE TO THE GRAND MASTER.

ABOVE Early Templars in battle dress. Two Knights were often shown on one horse to signify their vow of poverty.

garments. This was considered a superior position within the Order. Commanders were responsible for all Templar lands and properties, while Provincial Masters managed revenue and recruited new men. The Commanders each had a personal retinue of two squires, two foot soldiers, one sergeant, one deacon and one Saracen scribe. Like the Draper and the Marshals, most Commanders had four horses at their command as well as one palfrey (riding horse). Commanders of knights, houses and farms (also known as Casals) were responsible for the daily business of the various estates under their care. Casals were usually knights, but if no knight resided in the region, the position could go to a sergeant. If the Commander was a knight he was allowed four horses, but if a sergeant he was allowed only two.

THE HIGHER RANKS

A group of senior officials helped organize and run the Order efficiently. The Marshal had responsibility for military decisions and next in line to him were the Under Marshal, in charge of footmen and equipment, the Standard Bearer, who carried the Order's black and white banner, and the Draper, who was responsible for all Templars'

INITIATION INTO THE ORDER

The confidential Templar initiation ceremony often gave rise to suspicion because of its mystery. The ceremony always took place in a chapter, a local branch of the fraternity, and any disclosure of this incurred expulsion from the Order. Initiation was undertaken in secret because of the personal questions that were asked. During the rite, the vows would be taken and recruits signed over all their wealth and worldly goods. Naturally enough, it was this very secrecy that made some others wary of the Templars.

LEFT An imposing twelfth-century Templar castle in Ponferrada, Spain. King Fernando II of León placed this flourishing settlement under the custody of the Order of the Temple in 1178. The Knights Templar used the site of a primitive Roman fortress to build a castle in which they settled and which, at the same time, protected the passing pilgrims.

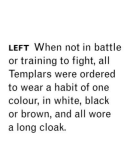

ABOVE A cloister in the twelfth-century church of St John the Baptist in Treviso, Italy. The curved Templar cross *pattée* carved in relief on the wall indicates Templar presence at its construction.

THE LOWER RANKS

Most of the Order's military power came from the knights and sergeants. Knights were usually of noble birth and wore the familiar white mantle with red cross. Each knight was permitted one squire and three horses. Sergeants did not have to be of noble birth and wore a black or brown mantle. They were given one horse and were required to be their own squires. Knights were forbidden from surrendering in battle, which, coupled with their belief in their salvation in Heaven, gave them a fearless and uncompromising nature. The serving brothers administered the Order's property and the rural brothers performed menial tasks and trades. Finally, the chaplains were ordained priests who saw to the spiritual needs of the Order.

With the high demand for fighting men, some knights signed up for a set period of time before returning to secular life. The majority of the Templars were both uneducated and illiterate (as were most knights of the day), having come not from the upper nobility, but from more ordinary backgrounds. Those who were educated were often employed in banking.

LEFT When not in battle or training to fight, all Templars were ordered to wear a habit of one colour, in white, black or brown, and all wore a long cloak.

A GROWING IDENTITY

AS THE TEMPLARS GREW FROM BEING THE ORIGINAL NINE SOLDIER MONKS SWORN TO POVERTY, CHASTITY, PIETY AND OBEDIENCE (OBEYING GOD AND THE GRAND MASTER), INTO WHAT ESSENTIALLY BECAME A MULTINATIONAL CORPORATION, SO TOO DID THEIR ORGANIZATION EVOLVE, REFLECTING ITS EXPANDING ROLE IN THE AFFAIRS OF THE HOLY LAND.

RIGHT Illustration of the four leaders of the First Crusade by Gustave Doré (1832–83), a popular nineteenth-century book illustrator, whose work showed a romantic view of the medieval battles.

Although their vow of poverty meant that they owned nothing personally, the Templars' resources grew as the Order flourished, and by the 1150s, a Grand Master had at his disposal four horses, two knights, a sergeant, a chaplain, a turcopole,

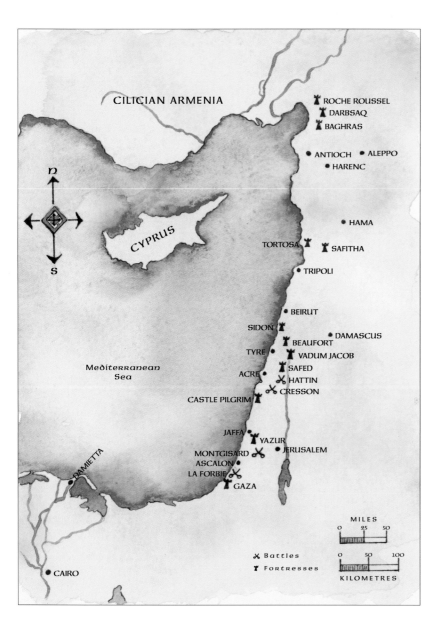

a farrier, a cook and a Saracen scribe. The Grand Masters had first choice when a new batch of horses arrived from the West.

Through their coherent structure, the Templars were able to grow and expand as a powerful and influential concern. They became one of the most extraordinary brotherhoods that ever existed: elite and unique warriors, unparalleled entrepreneurs,

LEFT The Holy Land during the Crusader period, showing Templar fortresses and the location of significant battles.

yet devoted men of God. As individuals, they stood apart with their distinctive white, brown or black mantles, emblazoned red crosses, and beards when most other men were smooth-cheeked; as an association, they prized their independence and their individual way of doing things. They often pursued their own strategies for success in their mission to protect the Holy Land and all Christian pilgrims.

TOLERANCE AND INTOLERANCE

For decades, the Templars had pursued a cautious policy in the East. This policy included making treaties with Islamic leaders, which made other orders suspicious of them, especially when they negotiated with the leader of the Assassins, a fervent Shiite sect. Yet, the Templars had no qualms in implementing any policy that strengthened their position as upholders of safety, law and order in Outremer. They were not just professional soldiers, but also diplomatic and political defenders of the frontier. Although for the vast majority of Christians, an alliance with any Muslim was unthinkable, the Templars knew that tolerance was necessary. This was a particularly intolerant time and their behaviour was out of step with the rest of the world. Yet the Templars were pragmatic; they were living on a frontier and they had daily contact with their Muslim neighbours; they were not in a position to wage perpetual war. However, this meant that rumours spread that they fraternized with the enemy.

FRUGAL EXISTENCE

Despite amassing vast wealth and creating such a powerful and disciplined organization, the Templars lived in a state of abstinence and self-denial, where individual identity was forbidden. They had to sleep in a shirt and breeches, with the light on, ate their two meals a day in silence, were forbidden to argue or to gossip and had no worldly comforts. Outside the capital cities or the territories where they were at war, they did not spend large sums on great castles or magnificent churches; their preceptories, barns, stables and dormitories, for instance, were modestly built for practicality.

LEFT *Creating a Templar* by A. Sanquirico and G. Bramatti. This nineteenth-century painting depicts a romanticized view of the Templar initiation ceremony.

BELOW Round church in Nyker, on Bornholm Island, Denmark. This is one of several round churches built by the Templars in Denmark during the twelfth century. The cone-shaped roof was not added until several centuries later.

SACRIFICIAL LIFESTYLE

Recruited in Europe and sent to the front line in the Holy Land, a Knight Templar soon became hardened to the austere conditions of the Order in the East. As monks of the Catholic Church, they were accustomed to strict discipline and their every moment, awake and asleep, was regulated. Each day involved prayer, work and training for battle; there was no leisure time. By joining the Order, Templars believed they were purifying themselves of the corruption and temptation of the world. Their lives were full of sacrifice, dedication and humility.

PIONEERS OF BANKING

QUITE EARLY IN THEIR HISTORY, THE TEMPLARS GAINED A REPUTATION FOR BEING RELIABLE BANKERS. IN EFFECT, THEY CREATED AND ESTABLISHED MODERN BANKING. AS RELIGIOUS MEN, TEMPLARS CONSIDERED THE IMMORTAL SOUL TO BE ABOVE THE TRANSITORY LIFE ON EARTH, SO THEY WERE EXCEPTIONALLY TRUSTWORTHY. THEY USED THE IMMENSE WEALTH THAT WAS ASSIGNED TO THEM WITH SKILL AND WISDOM, MAKING SIGNIFICANT INVESTMENTS IN LAND, AGRICULTURE AND INDUSTRY. IT COULD BE ARGUED THAT THEY PROVIDED THE INGREDIENTS FOR THE EXPANSION IN BUILDING THAT BEGAN TO CHANGE THE FACE OF EUROPE DURING THE MIDDLE AGES.

BELOW Prince Richard I of Capua making a donation to the Abbey of St Angelo in Formis, from a twelfth-century manuscript. This shows the regular practice of making donations to monasteries and churches during the Middle Ages.

By lending vast sums of money to destitute monarchs, the Templars became the bankers for every throne in Europe, and even for some Muslim rulers. As time passed, French monarchs, in particular, came to rely on their services, often bringing the Order close to bankruptcy. By the reign of Philip II (1180–1223), the Templars were effectively the French royal treasury and also lent money to the Church to finance ecclesiastical building programmes.

With so many preceptories (monastic houses) throughout Europe and the Holy Land, Templars also arranged, at modest interest rates, the safe and efficient transfer of money for merchant traders, who also became increasingly dependent on them. They developed a system of credit notes that could be given at one Templar preceptory and cashed at another. Templar buildings were so well fortified that they were impregnable – another reason for individuals to feel secure leaving their money in them. The Paris Temple became the major Templar financial base.

Using their own considerable commercial insights as well as the system of credit notes, they also developed the equivalent of safety deposit boxes and bankers' and travellers' cheques. Pilgrims were wary of carrying large sums of money as they travelled, so they deposited enough cash at local Templar preceptories to cover their estimated costs of travel, accommodation, and such things as alms and gift-giving. In return for the cash deposit, Templar treasurers gave each pilgrim a coded receipt. As they travelled, pilgrims handed in their receipts to local Templar treasurers who paid any of their dues, re-coded the receipt accordingly, and returned it to its owner.

BELOW Portrait of Guillaume d'Argenteuil, a Templar Treasurer. Pilgrims could travel without the encumbrance of money, using a coded chit issued by the Treasurer, a precursor to the traveller's cheque.

RIGHT Eleventh-century fresco from a Cistercian Abbey in Italy shows St Nicholas appearing to shipwrecked pilgrims. The Templars became viewed by many pilgrims as being as protective as St Nicholas himself.

When the trip was over, pilgrims presented their receipts to the Templar treasurer who had first issued it. Any balance of credit would be returned in cash, or if the pilgrim had overspent, he would be presented with the appropriate bill.

MONEY-LENDING

At the time, it was forbidden for Christians to charge interest on loans and therefore money-lending as a profession had been traditionally restricted to Jews. The Templars found a way around this. As they were allowed to charge rent for leasing a house or land, they used the same principle and charged "rent" rather than interest for their services. The rent was payable at the time the loan was granted and was added to the capital sum borrowed.

PUBLIC SERVANTS

Among the financial services provided by the Templars was the provision of pensions and annuities. People often donated land or money, but kept it for their lifetime. This ensured the salvation of the donor's soul and allowed them Templar protection. The function as a sort of police force had been visualized by Hugues de Payens; it now extended beyond the defence of pilgrims in Outremer to protecting the public and their money. In serving the rich and poor in this way, the Templars were becoming very important indeed.

LEFT Examples of eleventh and twelfth-century coins. The gold augustalis on the left was produced by Frederick, Holy Roman Emperor and King of Sicily, Germany, Brindisi and Messina (1194–1250). The back of a gold Byzantine coin on the right, dated 1025, shows Jesus Christ.

TEMPLAR ARCHITECTURE

SOON AFTER THE FORMATION OF THE ORDER, A NEW STYLE OF CHURCH ARCHITECTURE BEGAN APPEARING ACROSS WESTERN EUROPE. THE FIRST EXAMPLES WERE IN FRANCE, WHERE SOARING CATHEDRALS ARE EVIDENCE OF THE GOTHIC TRADITION. IT IS POSSIBLE THAT THE TEMPLARS WERE INVOLVED IN THE FINANCING AND CONSTRUCTION OF SOME OF THESE CATHEDRALS. WITH CHARTRES CATHEDRAL, FOR INSTANCE, THERE HAD TO BE A MASSIVE AND IMMEDIATE INPUT OF FINANCIAL RESOURCES TO PAY FOR THE QUARRYING AND TRANSPORT OF STONE AND THE ENORMOUS NUMBER OF STONEMASONS AND CRAFTSMEN NEEDED TO BUILD IT AT SUCH SPEED.

RIGHT Chartres Cathedral in France, one of the greatest of all Gothic cathedrals. On the doors and porches are many detailed carved figures holding swords, crosses and trade tools.

BELOW The nave of the cathedral of St Pierre and St Paul in Troyes, France. The airy Gothic arches echoed throughout emanate an uplifting experience.

In line with everything they did, the Templars understood and appreciated the value of sound architectural practice from early on. Because their only authority was the Pope, they were able to explore and experiment as they chose. When developing their financial acumen they drew on ideas from those around them. Similarly, they acquired expert building techniques from the diverse cultures they lived among. Their architects and masons were the best around.

In addition, they employed local workmen who used vernacular materials, styles and techniques. It is also claimed that the Templars based many of their buildings on the measurements of an ancient geometric system.

The Templars had been involved with building from their inception. When Baldwin II gave them quarters in the al-Aqsa mosque, he also gave them complete freedom to develop the area as they wanted. They used Temple Mount as their

headquarters from 1119 to 1187, when Saladin reclaimed it and converted it back into a mosque, and they based many of their later churches on the "Templum Solomonis" or "Templum Domini".

TEMPLAR CHURCHES

In 1139, Pope Innocent II granted the Order a unique privilege – the right to build their own churches and to have their own consecrated graveyards. One of their building characteristics in Europe was the church with a round nave, modelled on Temple Mount. Not all Templar churches had round naves, nor did all churches with round naves originate with the Templars, but they are associated with them. Temple Church in London is one of the finest examples of a round church in Europe.

The fashion for round naves died out by the late thirteenth century and there was a general rebuilding of churches, when the curved Romanesque apses and round naves were squared off. The majority of Templar churches are small, undecorated rectangular buildings, complying with St Bernard's original instructions for simple architecture. In the main, Templar churches

remained modest in comparison to the Gothic cathedrals and abbeys of the same period. In some areas, Templar churches began to look more like fortified manors. Nevertheless, they decorated these churches lavishly inside to please God; with painted arches, silver, gilt and ivory candlesticks and vessels, vibrantly painted frescoes and richly coloured banners. Originally, burials with effigies were not allowed inside Templar churches, but the London Temple shows how this was eventually forgotten. Rich patrons were laid to rest within the church, often under elaborately carved canopies.

LEFT Interior of Rosslyn Chapel, Scotland. Rosslyn Chapel seems to be ironically connected with the Templars, since it was built over 100 years after their suppression. Outside, the Chapel looks like other fifteenth-century churches with flying buttresses and gables, but inside, every wall is encrusted with fantastic carvings and decoration.

LEFT The oldest part of Temple Church, London, modelled after the Temple of Solomon. Building began in 1166 and was completed in February 1185. It was dedicated to the Virgin Mary and consecrated by the Patriarch of Jerusalem. In the Templars' time it was full of colour, light and sound, with Masses said at all hours of the day. Part of it was carpeted and hung with banners, giving it a feeling of opulence.

BUILDING FOR POSTERITY

THE TEMPLARS BECAME PROLIFIC BUILDERS. THEY BUILT AND MAINTAINED FORTIFIED CASTLES, FARMS, OUTBUILDINGS, BARNS, STABLES AND CHURCHES, AND THEY WERE PARTICULARLY SKILLED AT BUILDING ON CHALLENGING GROUND, SUCH AS SAND OR MARSH. THEY EVEN BUILT ENTIRE TOWNS SUCH AS BALDOCK IN HERTFORDSHIRE, WHICH WAS FOUNDED BY THE TEMPLARS BETWEEN 1199 AND 1254. IT BECAME THEIR ENGLISH HEADQUARTERS AND IS BELIEVED TO BE NAMED AFTER BAGHDAD OR PERHAPS BALD OAK, WHICH MEANS DEAD OAK, AS THEY NEVER ACTUALLY OCCUPIED BAGHDAD.

RIGHT St Thyrse, a twelfth-century Templar church in the Champagne region of France demonstrates the norm for Templar churches – modest rectangular buildings with little or no decoration.

BELOW Almourol Castle, a Templar stronghold in Portugal. The Knights Templar were also responsible for the defence of the ancient capital, Coimbra. They rebuilt the castle and completed it in 1171.

As in every Templar endeavour, quality and practicality were of paramount importance. Like the Cistercians, the Templars sought functionality rather than beauty and the building techniques of their early structures show a strong influence of Norman architecture. Walls were usually faced with the best quality stone and in-filled with rubble set in strong mortar. Regional preceptories, such as Temple Garway in Herefordshire, were simple, plain and durable buildings, while castles, such as Athlit near Haifa and Tortosa in Tripoli, were the pinnacle of medieval military architecture.

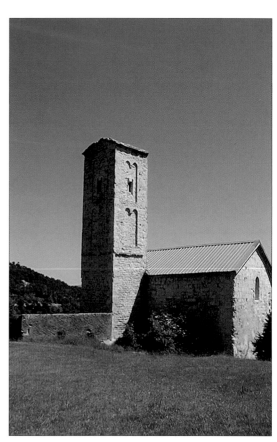

TOWERS OF STONE

Even though all Templar fortresses looked extremely forbidding and were practically impregnable, Athlit was the only Templar castle never to be taken by the enemy. In the final crusades, Templar castles spread across Europe – towering stone fortresses that were strongholds on the outside, but resembled monasteries within. Others adopted Templar building innovations over the next few centuries. Most castles, whether built

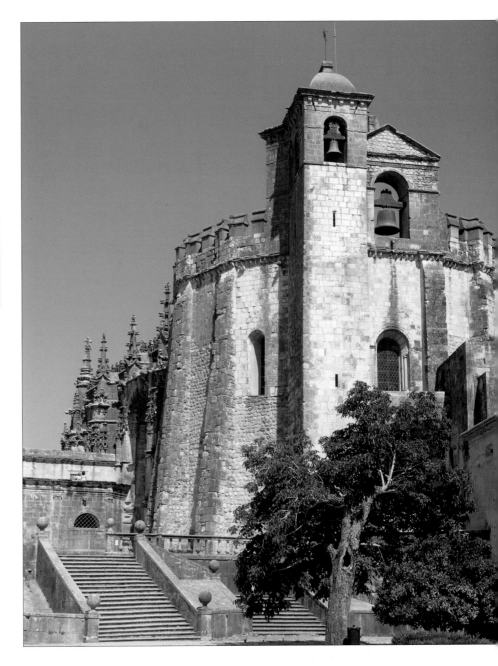

MIXED STYLES

Templar buildings were often an inventive amalgam of Roman, Byzantine, Islamic and European influences. They employed a diversity of styles from Romanesque architecture. Their European-type towers not only created an impressive exterior silhouette, but added strength and impregnability to fortresses, and their domes added Byzantine beauty to places of worship. The most notable influence of the Islamic world on Templar buildings and, in turn, the whole of Christian Europe was the introduction of the pointed arch, with which Muslim architects were well acquainted.

from scratch or refurbished by the Templars, such as Almourol and Tomar in Portugal, were often in the shape of a quadrangle, protected by circular towers along the walls. Several of their fortresses were constructed with deep moats within double walls. One Templar innovation was the jail tower, built in the centre of the quadrangle.

DURABILITY AND PERMANENCE

The enduring values of Templar life are summed up by the physical durability of their buildings – whether churches, castles or preceptories. The Knights Templar were realistic men living in an intolerant world. They knew about the practicalities of life better than any other organization of their time, and they responded accordingly. That so many of their buildings are still to be found (and many churches are still in use) proves the reliability of their techniques and the resilience of their craftsmanship. For example, the Chastel Blanc (known as the white tower) in Syria was built by the Order on existing fortifications. Constructed with limestone blocks, the tower survived an earthquake in 1202 while all buildings around it fell. At the height of the Templars' powers, they owned over 3,000 donated properties in Europe, which they adapted with their own fortifications.

ABOVE Convent of Christ Castle in Tomar, Portugal, built in 1160 by Gualdim Pais, provincial Master Templar there during 1156–95. The convent was built as a stronghold and was based on the Dome of the Rock in Jerusalem, that is, a 16-sided polygon.

LEFT Illumination on vellum (1270) of the construction of the Abbey of St Genevieve, which shows how Templar building was prolific from the eleventh to fourteenth centuries.

MILITARY DISCIPLINE

THE TEMPLARS WERE EXTREMELY WELL DISCIPLINED. THEY HAD RULES ABOUT PRACTICALLY EVERYTHING IN THEIR LIVES, FROM HOW THEY ATE TO WHAT LENGTH THEIR BEARDS SHOULD BE. NOTORIOUSLY FEARED BY THEIR ENEMIES, THEIR COMBATIVE STATUS WAS UNRIVALLED. THEY HAD NO FEAR OF DEATH IN BATTLE BECAUSE THEY BELIEVED THEY WOULD BE GRANTED ETERNAL SALVATION. IT WAS SAID THAT TEMPLARS NEVER ASKED HOW MANY THE ENEMY NUMBERED, JUST WHERE THEY WERE. THEY WERE THE FIRST TO ARRIVE AT A BATTLE AND THE LAST TO LEAVE, AND THEY WERE RESPECTED BY GREAT WARRIORS SUCH AS SALADIN AND RICHARD THE LIONHEART.

RIGHT Crusading Knights from the Battle of Ascalon, 18 November 1177, when King Baldwin IV of Jerusalem gained control of the entire Palestine coast.

BELOW Templars in battle were known for their heroic prowess, chivalry, courage and discipline. Since they spent most of their time training, when actually fighting they were usually the most determined warriors.

The Templars utilized both cavalry and infantry. Their cavalry were not only skilled in archery on horseback, but their huge steeds were also trained to bite and kick and the infantry were skilled in the use of axes and spears. The Templars' primary tactic was the cavalry charge. First, the infantry provided cover, and then the cavalry charged, annihilating everything in its path. The Templars' flying black and white banner would allow them to easily regroup in order to continue the attack. They never left the battlefield while the banner remained upright and if it was lost to view, they

joined with another group of allies. The banner was held by the Marshal and ten knights were assigned to guard it, while one kept a spare banner furled on his lance.

TEMPLAR HORSES

The care of horses was of prime importance. Templars' horses were the closest they had to owning anything and they were extremely expensive. There were several different types of horse: great warhorses for knights; lighter, speedier mounts for the turcopoles; palfreys for lightweight riding; packhorses and mules. Horses were bred on stud farms in Jerusalem and Europe, particularly in France and Spain. As with the rest of their duties, there were

LEFT The siege of Antioch lasted from 21 October 1097 to 3 June 1098, during the First Crusade, and became legendary by the twelfth century. This painting shows the fighting between Christians and Muslims just outside the city walls.

BELOW The assassination of Thomas à Becket, Archbishop of Canterbury (1118–70) by Henry II's own knights. The knights' punishment for the crime was to serve with the extremely disciplined Templars. Henry donated money to the Order.

strict regulations about looking after the horses. They were of paramount importance and one of the only excusable reasons for missing prayers was if a knight was tending to a horse. Some Templars were assigned their own horse or horses, but the rest were in a "pool" so everyone had responsibility for them. Many knights brought their own steeds with them when they joined the Order.

TEMPLAR COLLABORATION

The Templars' military professionalism proved itself many times. In battle, they would sustain combat where others would concede defeat. The element of surprise was another strong tactic. By 1177, for various reasons, there was discord among the Christian rulers in Outremer. Saladin, taking advantage of this, led a force across the Sinai Desert towards the Templar fortress of Gaza. The Templars concentrated their forces to defend it but Saladin avoided it and laid siege to Ascalon. Baldwin IV raised an army to defend Ascalon and Saladin, realizing that Jerusalem was undefended, marched towards the Holy City. Baldwin summoned the Templars from Gaza and they surprised Saladin and his unsuspecting army. With only a tenth of his men remaining, Saladin fled back to Egypt.

THE MURDER OF THOMAS À BECKET

The Templars tried to resolve the misunderstanding between Henry II and the Archbishop of Canterbury, Thomas à Becket but they were, of course, unsuccessful. Four royal knights carried out Henry's command to murder the priest in Canterbury Cathedral on 29 December 1170. The penance imposed on them for the murder was to serve 14 years with the Templars in the Holy Land. Henry also promised to provide the Templars with money to support 200 knights for a year, demonstrating the awe and respect that the Templars commanded.

THE SECOND CRUSADE

ON CHRISTMAS EVE IN 1144, THE CITY OF EDESSA FELL TO AN ARMY UNDER IMAD AD-DIN ZENGI, GOVERNOR OF MOSUL. WHEN THE NEWLY ELECTED POPE EUGENIUS III HEARD OF IT THE FOLLOWING AUTUMN, HE WROTE TO LOUIS VII OF FRANCE, ASKING HIM TO LEAD A CRUSADE TO RECOVER EDESSA. YET, LOUIS WAS UNPOPULAR, AS THREE YEARS EARLIER HE HAD ILLEGALLY SEIZED LANDS FROM THEOBALD OF CHAMPAGNE. REALIZING HE WAS WITHOUT ALLIES, HE TURNED TO A MAN WHO HAD BOTH AUTHORITY AND RESPECT – BERNARD OF CLAIRVAUX.

RIGHT Louis VII (1120–80) was the first European monarch to take up the challenge of a crusade. In 1146, he responded to Pope Eugenius' call to arms and left for the Holy Land the following year.

As a compelling preacher and great diplomat, Bernard of Clairvaux had built up a unique position as the adviser of popes and kings. He had links with Eugenius III and Louis VII's brother Henri, who were both monks at Clairvaux, and he was instrumental in reconciling Louis VII with Theobald of Champagne.

THE MEETINGS

On 31 March 1146, huge crowds gathered at Vézelay to hear Bernard preach the Crusade. So many turned up that Bernard had to stand on a specially constructed platform. By the time he finished speaking, thousands wanted to join the Crusade and Louis was the first to pledge his allegiance. Bernard travelled around France,

BELOW Louis VII leaving France for the Second Crusade, 1147–9. St Bernard of Clairvaux can be seen preaching in the bottom right-hand corner.

preaching that the soul of everyone who fought this Crusade would be saved. The army grew rapidly. Eugenius asked Bernard to persuade the reluctant King Conrad III of Germany to join. Bernard used his well-known powers of persuasion and Conrad took the Cross. On 27 April 1147, Louis, Eugenius, Bernard, four archbishops and about 260 Templars attended a meeting in Paris about the Second Crusade. It was at this meeting that Eugenius probably granted the Order authorization to wear the splayed red cross.

TEMPLAR CONTROL

Everard des Barres, Grand Master between 1146 and 1149, became one of Louis' most trusted advisers. The German army had gone ahead to the Holy Land and the French were disheartened to

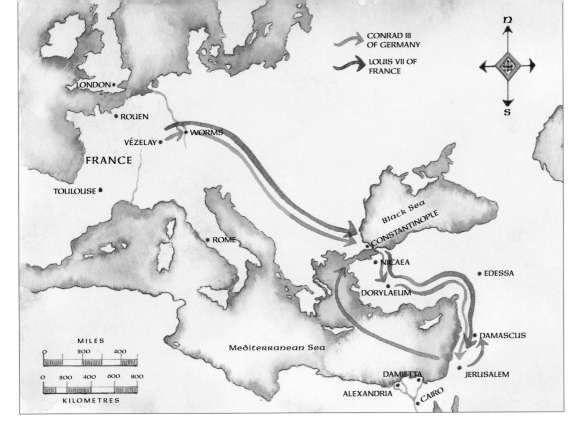

CONRAD III
OF GERMANY

LOUIS VII OF
FRANCE

LONDON

ROUEN

VÉZELAY • WORMS

FRANCE

TOULOUSE

ROME

Black Sea

CONSTANTINOPLE

NICAEA

DORYLAEUM

EDESSA

DAMASCUS

MILES

200   400

Mediterranean Sea

200   400   600   800

DAMIETTA

JERUSALEM

KILOMETRES

ALEXANDRIA   CAIRO

LEFT Map showing the routes of the Second Crusade. The armies of the French and German kings marched across Europe separately and were delayed by the Byzantine Emperor at Constantinople. The Germans were defeated by the Turks at Dorylaeum, and Conrad fled back to Nicaea, remaining there until the French arrived. Louis and Conrad and their diminished armies reached Jerusalem and in 1148 participated in a misguided attack on Damascus.

hear of their defeat at Dorylaeum by the Turks. The Franks' heavy cavalry was useless, while the Turks were masters of archery from the saddle, so Everard divided the army into smaller units, each led by a Templar knight, to provide greater control.

Eventually, Louis and Conrad reached Jerusalem and resolved to besiege Damascus. The siege proceeded extremely slowly, so the leaders moved the Crusaders to a new position. This turned out to be disastrous as there was no water supply, so the siege was abandoned. All sides felt betrayed by each other. Conrad returned to Constantinople, while Louis remained in Jerusalem. The hopes of the Crusade dwindled and the straggling armies returned home.

Louis VII later wrote that it was the Templars alone who prevented the Second Crusade from deteriorating into a complete disaster. Political divisions among most of the Crusaders were in sharp contrast to the greater unity among the Muslims, excepting the Templars, whose strategy was always to work together in harmony. When Louis had exhausted his funds in the journey across Asia Minor, Everard des Barres provided the solution once again. On 10 May 1148, he sailed from Antioch to Acre, where he raised sufficient capital to fund the rest of the Crusade.

Ultimately though, the Second Crusade had failed. As soon as the outcome was known back in Europe, there was a widespread reaction against crusading as a major mission. There were recriminations for everyone and no one really understood why there had been so much activity for so little result. The armed pilgrimage had not lost its allure, nor the promise of remission of sins, but confidence had been knocked.

BELOW Louis VII taking the banner at St Denis in 1147. Pope Eugenius III is handing him the staff and the King's wife, Eleanor of Aquitaine, is kneeling in prayer at his side. The Pope gives his blessing for the Second Crusade.

SALADIN

SALAH AL-DIN YUSUF BIN AYUB, OR SALADIN AS HE IS POPULARLY KNOWN, WAS BORN IN 1138 AND OF KURDISH DESCENT. HIS NAME MEANS "RIGHTEOUSNESS OF THE FAITH". AN INTELLIGENT CHILD, AT 14 HE WAS SENT TO DAMASCUS TO FINISH HIS EDUCATION. HE ENTERED INTO THE SERVICE OF NOUR ED-DIN, A GREAT ARAB WARRIOR AND THE SECOND SON OF IMAD AD-DIN ZENGI, WHO HAD OVERTHROWN EDESSA IN 1144. IT WAS NOUR ED-DIN'S DREAM TO UNITE THE VARIOUS MUSLIM FORCES TO CREATE A COMMON FORCE AGAINST THE CHRISTIANS. NOUR ED-DIN ALSO CONSTRUCTED UNIVERSITIES AND MOSQUES IN ALL THE CITIES HE CONTROLLED.

In 1171, the caliph of Baghdad died and Saladin ruled Egypt, but as Nour ed-Din's representative. He was authoritative and effective, being literate, cultured and skilled in warfare and weaponry.

After the death of Nour ed-Din in 1174, Saladin proclaimed himself the sultan of Egypt and began his expansion of territories. In 12 years, he had Damascus, Syria, Aleppo and Iraq in his possession.

FIGHTING THE CRUSADERS

In 1178, the Templars began constructing a castle to destabilize Saladin's empire – the fortress of Jacob's Ford. The castle was designed to be a

ABOVE Twentieth-century painting of Saladin (1138–93) entering Jerusalem in October 1187 after he had recaptured it.

RIGHT Nineteenth-century artist's impression of Saladin, shrewd statesman and great commander of the Muslims during the twelfth century. He founded the Ayyubid dynasty of Egypt, Syria, Yemen, Iraq, Mecca Hejaz and Diyar Bakr.

Saladin soon began to stand out among Nour ed-Din's forces. In 1169 he served with Nour ed-Din's trusted general and with his own uncle, Shirkuh. Saladin and Shirkuh thwarted the attempt of King Amalric I of Jerusalem to invade Egypt. When Shirkuh died, Saladin succeeded him as vizier, a type of high-ranking minister, and faced the difficult role of defending Egypt against the Latin Kingdom of Jerusalem. No one expected Saladin to last long in this position as he was young and there was a history in Egypt of many changes of government, but he managed to switch Egyptian Muslims' spiritual allegiance from the caliph in Cairo to the caliph in Baghdad.

defensive tool as well as an offensive weapon, to severely inhibit Saladin's ability to invade the Christian kingdom while simultaneously undermining his security in Damascus. In 1179, Saladin began to prepare for a large-scale attack on the Crusader states, and Jacob's Ford was his first target. After five days of ferocious struggle, Saladin slaughtered more than half the garrison before dismantling the fort and abandoning the site. It has since been discovered that the fortress had not been finished and therefore was vulnerable. In 1187, Saladin recaptured Jerusalem at the Battle of Hattin near the Lake of Galilee. When his soldiers entered Jerusalem, he forbade them from robbing or killing civilians or damaging the city. It was his compassion as much as his fighting skills that spread his fame.

Devout and compassionate, among many other achievements Saladin built a citadel in Cairo. Within it was a spacious hospital staffed with doctors. It had special rooms, beds and servants to look after the sick, free food and medicine, and a separate ward for sick women. Nearby was another building with barred windows for the insane, who were treated humanely and cared for by experts who tried to find out what had happened to their minds – a modern attitude

COURTESY AND CRUELTY
During his lifetime, even Saladin's enemies recognized his courage and courtesy. Stories of his kindness spread. For instance, he gave furs to some of his Christian prisoners for warmth in the dungeons of Damascus and he withheld attack on the tower of Kerak Castle in Jordan as a Christian wedding was taking place there. However, he could also be cruel. He had Shiite opponents crucified, for example, and often mutilated or executed his captives.

ABOVE Saladin and the Battle of Hattin, 1187. Saladin had ordered the attack on the crusading army at dawn. The Christians were weakened by thirst and the heat and were overcome. After Hattin, the Christians in the Holy Land seemed doomed.

LEFT Tenth-century watercolour painting of Arabs in combat with staffs. Saladin had told his men, "I shall purify the land of these impure races". He rewarded every soldier who had captured a Knight Templar with 50 dinar.

unheard of elsewhere. Saladin admired the chivalrous code of Christian knights, but had a ruthless hatred for military orders. He died in Damascus in 1193 at the age of 55.

RICHARD THE LIONHEART

RICHARD PLANTAGENET WAS KING OF ENGLAND FROM 1189 TO 1199, YET HE ONLY SPENT SIX MONTHS OF HIS REIGN THERE. HIS MOTHER WAS ELEANOR, QUEEN OF AQUITAINE, AND HE SPENT MUCH OF HIS YOUTH AT HER COURT. ELEANOR HAD BEEN MARRIED TO LOUIS VII OF FRANCE, BUT THEIR MARRIAGE WAS ANNULLED AFTER THE SECOND CRUSADE. EIGHT WEEKS LATER, AT THE AGE OF THIRTY, ELEANOR MARRIED THE 19-YEAR-OLD COUNT OF ANJOU, WHO BECAME HENRY II OF ENGLAND IN 1154. BETWEEN 1152 AND 1162, ELEANOR AND HENRY HAD FIVE SONS AND THREE DAUGHTERS.

ABOVE Richard I of England (1157–99), third son of Henry II. The troubadour Bertran de Born called him Oc-e-Non (Yes-and-No), while some later writers referred to him as Richard the Lionheart, Cœur de Lion.

joined Philip II of France (the son of his mother's ex-husband) against his father in 1188. Tall and fearless, he soon established his reputation as a ferocious warrior and brilliant strategist.

THE SALADIN TITHE

Prince Henry died of dysentery in 1183 and his brother Geoffrey died soon after, leaving Richard heir to the English throne. In 1187, Saladin conquered many states of the Holy Land and in 1189, Henry II died. On 3 September, Richard was crowned King of England in Westminster Abbey. Yet by December, he was planning to join the Third Crusade and he departed for Outremer in 1190 with Philip of France. To raise funds, Richard imposed a tax on the English people, which became known as "a Saladin tithe". The tithe was collected in each parish in the presence of the parish priest, a rural dean, a Knight Templar and others. Excommunication was the punishment for not paying.

Richard was her third and favourite son, who, at the age of 11, was declared Duke of Aquitaine, while his elder brother Henry waited to inherit the English crown. Richard cared more for his mother than his father and family considerations influenced much of his life. For instance, he fought alongside his elder brothers and mother in their rebellion of 1173–4 against his father Henry II of England; he fought with his father against his brothers when they supported an 1183 revolt in his mother's duchy of Aquitaine; and he

THE TEMPLARS AND THE LIONHEART

In 1191, Richard fought with the Templars against Saladin, nearly taking Jerusalem twice. The new Grand Master, Robert de Sablé, was Richard's good friend and their personalities complemented each other. The Templars fought alongside Richard throughout the Third Crusade, following Robert's cautious lead and Richard's intrepid tactics.

LEFT In 1189, following the death of Henry II, Richard was crowned King of England in Westminster Abbey, London. This painting shows his coronation procession.

BELOW Eleanor of Aquitaine, Richard's mother, Queen consort of both France and England in turn. One of Europe's most powerful women during the Middle Ages.

Meanwhile, Philip II returned to France after a row with Richard and schemed to put Richard's younger brother John on the English throne. Hearing of this, Richard decided to return home, but was captured by Leopold V of Austria and imprisoned by the Holy Roman Emperor, Henry VI. Released in 1194, he crushed a coup attempt by John and regained lands lost to Philip II during his captivity. Richard's war with Philip continued sporadically until 1198 and he died from a war wound on 6 April 1199.

THE CONQUERING OF CYPRUS

As Richard had journeyed to the Holy Land, one of his ships was wrecked off the Cyprus coast and another, carrying his betrothed, Berengaria of Navarre, and his sister Joan, was forced into the port of Limassol.

The self-appointed ruler of Cyprus, a rebel Byzantine prince, Isaac Ducas Comnenus, had formed an alliance with Saladin and captured the shipwrecked crusaders. When their release was not forthcoming, Richard, joined by nobles and Templars, swiftly conquered Cyprus. Ducas

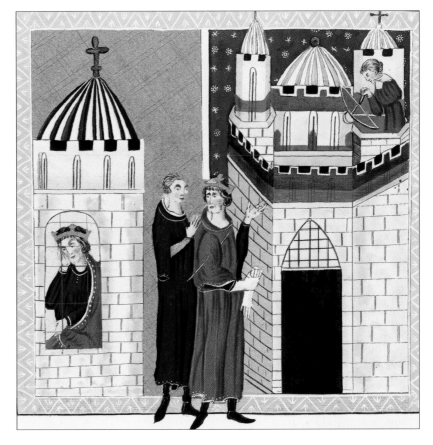

pleaded not to be clapped in irons, so Richard shackled him in silver instead. Later, Robert de Sablé bought the island of Cyprus from Richard for 25,000 silver marks.

ABOVE This thirteenth-century illustration shows Richard in prison in Vienna in 1192 (left), and wounded and killed in the Chalus castle siege.

THE THIRD CRUSADE

IN 1174, KING AMALRIC OF JERUSALEM DIED. AMALRIC HAD WEAKENED THE STRENGTH OF HIS KINGDOM WITH HIS FRUITLESS EXCURSIONS INTO EGYPT. HE WAS SUCCEEDED BY HIS 13-YEAR-OLD SON, BALDWIN IV, WHO WAS A LEPER. SOME PEOPLE BELIEVED THAT THIS LEPROSY WAS A PUNISHMENT FROM GOD BECAUSE HIS FATHER, AMALRIC, HAD MARRIED ONE OF HIS COUSINS. BALDWIN WAS EDUCATED BY THE TEMPLARS' CHRONICLER, GUILLAUME DE TYRE.

BELOW Crusaders fighting the Muslims at the Battle of Montgisard on 25 November 1177.

In November 1177, Baldwin and the Templars defeated Saladin at the Battle of Montgisard, in the Holy Land near Ramla, the capital city of the Muslims before Jerusalem. In 1178 and 1179, Baldwin fought with the Templars against Saladin. In August, the unfinished castle at Jacob's Ford fell to Saladin, and in March 1185, Baldwin died. In the dynastic dispute that followed, Gérard de Ridefort, the Grand Master, betrayed an oath made to Baldwin and consequently brought the European community in the Holy Land close to civil war. Then in July 1187, Ridefort led his

knights, along with the rest of the Christian army, into a catastrophic battle at Hattin (located between Acre and Jaffa on the map). The Christian forces were almost wiped out, and two months later, Jerusalem itself, captured nearly a century earlier, was again in Saracen hands.

TAKING UP THE CROSS
Europe was horrified and prepared for the Third Crusade, while the Templars remained in the East, protecting what was still in Christian control. In various skirmishes, several Templar castles fell but

RIGHT Route of the Third Crusade (1127–93). It began with Saladin winning the Battle of Hattin in 1187. In 1189, Emperor Frederick left Europe but drowned in Anatolia a year later. In July 1190, Philip of France and Richard of England left for the Holy Land. By July 1191, Acre was surrendered to the Crusaders, and Philip returned to France soon after. In 1191, Richard met Saladin at the Battle of Arsur, and in 1192 he returned to England.

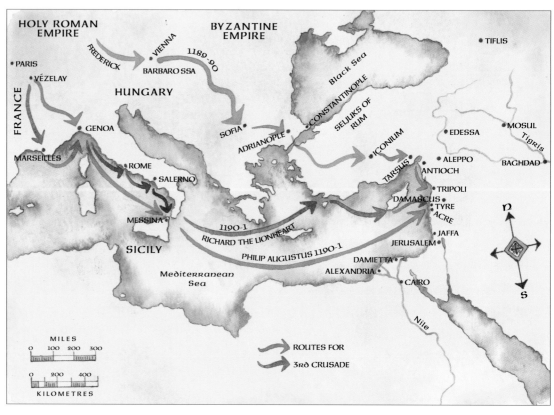

significant possessions remained. Then, in a bitter confrontation, the city of Acre fell and all seemed lost. The new Pope, Gregory VIII, proclaimed that the capture of Jerusalem was punishment for the sins of Christians across Europe. Henry II of England and Philip II of France ended their war with each other. In Britain, Baldwin the Archbishop of Canterbury made a tour through Wales, persuading 3,000 men-at-arms to take up the cross. Henry II died in 1189 and Richard I, who inherited the crown, immediately began raising funds for the crusade. Not only Richard and Philip, but the Emperor of the Holy Roman Empire, Frederick (called Barbarossa after his red beard), supported the Crusade, which is why it is sometimes called the Kings' Crusade.

RICHARD, SALADIN AND THE TEMPLARS

Richard utilized the discipline of the outnumbered Templars and they worked well together. He disposed the troops carefully and, for the first time since Hattin, defeated Saladin's army just outside Jerusalem at the Forest of Arsuf. The Templars then besieged Acre. On 12 July 1191, the Muslim occupying force surrendered. Richard moved into the royal palace and Philip into the fortress previously held by the Templars.

With Acre now in Christian hands, many crusaders returned home. Richard the Lionheart was left as the acknowledged leader of the crusading army. He established his new headquarters at Jaffa and began to negotiate with Saladin. But co-operation between the two factions was protracted. Richard returned to Acre just as Saladin made a surprise move against Jaffa, taking the town after three days. Richard, accompanied by only a small army (including Templars) retaliated and beat off the much larger

Muslim force. Negotiations concluded soon after this, with Richard agreeing to demolish Ascalon (west of Jerusalem) and Saladin agreeing to recognize Christian possessions along the coast. Christians and Muslims were to be allowed to cross each other's territory and Christian pilgrims were free to visit Jerusalem and all other Holy sites in Muslim hands. On 9 October 1192, Richard went back to England and never returned, while Saladin died the following March.

ABOVE Richard the Lionheart leads the Crusaders in battle against the Muslims at Arsur, north of Jaffa, in September 1191.

BELOW Twelfth-century Crusader propaganda. Richard I is unhorsing Saladin whose helmet is toppling off to reveal the features of the Devil.

OTHER ORDERS

THE TEMPLARS WERE NOT THE ONLY ORDER IN THE HOLY LAND. BECAUSE OF THE FERVOUR OF THE CRUSADES, SEVERAL OTHER CHRISTIAN ORDERS SPRANG UP, THE MOST IMPORTANT OF WHOM WERE THE KNIGHTS HOSPITALLERS. AT TIMES, SQUABBLES BETWEEN THE TEMPLARS AND THE HOSPITALLERS CAUSED PROBLEMS BETWEEN THE TWO ORDERS.

ABOVE A twentieth-century illustration of a Knight Hospitaller and a Knight Templar with two Christian pilgrims on either side of them. The image serves to show how the different Orders worked alongside each other much of the time.

RIGHT The thirteenth-century fortified castle of Malbork in Poland became the seat of the Teutonic Order from 1309. It is Europe's largest Gothic fortress and was meticulously restored in the nineteenth and early twentieth centuries.

The Knights Hospitallers, also known as the Order of St John of Jerusalem, the Knights of Rhodes or the Knights of Malta, had formed as a Benedictine order following the First Crusade in around 1070. It was founded by a group of merchants from Amalfi. Like the Templars, they were charged with the care and defence of Christian pilgrims in Palestine, but unlike them, they were not a military order, rather a lay community devoted to the care of poor pilgrims. Wearing a black mantle with a white cross, they worked and fought in conjunction with the Templars and these soon became the two most powerful Christian groups in the area.

By the mid-twelfth century, the Hospitallers divided between military brothers and those who cared for the sick. Like the Templars, the Hospitallers were exempt from all authority apart from the Pope, did not have to pay tithes and had their own substantial buildings. At the height of the kingdom of Jerusalem, the Hospitallers held seven great forts and 140 other estates in the area. They built their first hospice on the site where it was believed the conception of St John the Baptist had been announced by an angel.

THE TEUTONIC ORDER

After the Third Crusade, a new military order was established in the Holy Land. In 1197, German crusaders had arrived in Outremer; they were not particularly successful in their endeavours to retrieve parts of the Holy Land for Christianity and many returned home. A number of knights

LEFT *Krak des Chevaliers* ("Castle of the Knights" in a mixture of Arabic and French) in Syria, stands 2,300 feet above sea level. It is considered the greatest fortress in the world. The original had been built in 1031 for the Emir of Aleppo and was captured by Crusaders in 1099 during the First Crusade. In 1144, Raymond II, Count of Tripoli, gave it to the Knights Hospitallers.

BELOW The Order of the Knights of Calatrava was a Spanish order created in 1155 by Diego Velázquez, a monk who had been a knight.

BELOW Engraving of the Grand Master Knights Hospitallers, founded in Jerusalem in around 1070 to care for sick pilgrims. Initially the Order just cared for the pilgrims in Jerusalem but it soon began providing an armed escort to pilgrims.

remained, however, and joined a field hospital that had been set up in 1190 by merchants from Bremen and Lübeck to care for their sick and wounded. Their first base in Acre was a tent made of a ship's mainsail. They soon formed an order of knights, which became called the Teutonic Order, adopted the Templar Rule and wore white habits but with a black cross instead of red.

SMALLER ORDERS

Several smaller orders were active in the Holy Land. The Hospital of St Lazarus was founded after the Hospitallers and the Templars. Set up for knights who became affected with leprosy, it is believed to have originated from a Greek or Armenian leper house in Jerusalem. During the early 1100s, it was taken over by the Hospital of St John, which set up a chain of houses for lepers across Palestine and Europe, known as "Lazar Houses". The Templar Rule stipulated that any brother who contracted leprosy had to transfer to the Order of St Lazarus.

The Knights of Our Lady of Montjoie was founded by a Spanish knight, Count Rodrigo,

and named after the castle of Montjoie, just outside Jerusalem. It was recognized by the Pope in 1180. Rodrigo gave the Order lands in Castile and Aragon and the King of Jerusalem gave them several towers to garrison in Ascalon. Unfortunately, there was trouble with recruitment and in 1187, Montjoie changed its name to the Order of Trufac. In 1221, Fernando of Aragon ordered it to be merged with the Knights of Calatrava.

The Hospitallers of St Thomas of Canterbury (or Knights of St Thomas Acon), were founded around the same time as the Teutonic Order. They began as a hospital for Englishmen and were militarized around the time of the Fifth Crusade.

PART FOUR

FALL AND TRIAL

 During the thirteenth century, the situation in the Holy Land worsened. Outremer was under Muslim control. The Templars fought valiantly, but were unsuccessful. With the loss of Outremer, they had lost their prime purpose. Making their new headquarters in Cyprus, they turned their interests to Europe and started to explore fresh areas of knowledge such as innovative farming methods and skills in medicine. They had by then acquired, and built on, large tracts of land, bought farms and vineyards, become involved in manufacturing, importing and exporting, owned their own fleet of ships and for a time even the island of Cyprus. Their understanding of many modern ideas was so far advanced that rumours circulated about their "singular" notions. Certain people, jealous of their expertise and money-making prowess, and suspicious of their amity with Arabs and Jews, began to watch them warily.

RIGHT This illustration from the *Speculum Majus*, an important thirteenth-century encyclopedia, shows the fall of Acre in 1291 and the return of Philip II to France. Acre was surrounded by a great wall supported by ten towers. The Muslims attacked it with many siege towers and catapults and tunnelled at the fortifications below.

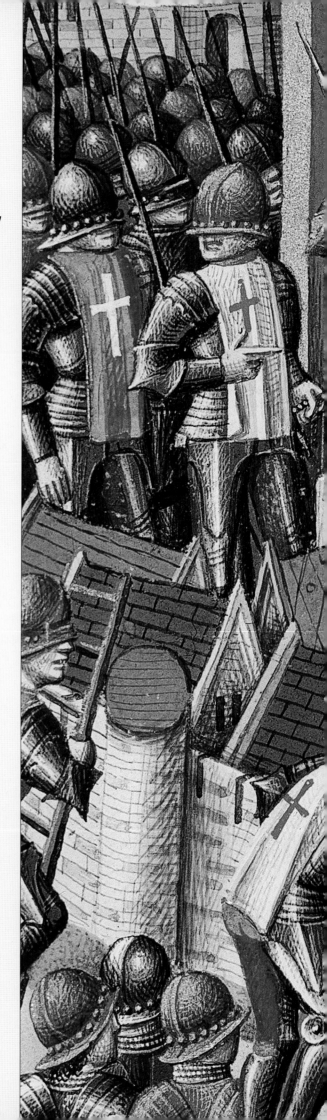

THE LAST CRUSADES

DURING THE FOURTEENTH CENTURY, THE HOLY LAND REMAINED IN A STATE OF FLUX. AFTER THE FAILURE OF THE THIRD CRUSADE, THERE WAS LITTLE INTEREST IN EUROPE FOR ANOTHER. POPE INNOCENT III COMMISSIONED THE FOURTH CRUSADE – THE LAST OF THE CRUSADES TO BE DIRECTED BY THE POPE. IN 1202, THE ARMY PLANNED TO LEAVE VENICE BY SEA AND ATTACK EGYPT BEFORE HEADING TO JERUSALEM. IN 1204, CRUSADERS SACKED CONSTANTINOPLE, THE MAJOR THOROUGHFARE TO THE EAST, AND NEVER MADE IT TO PALESTINE, SO THE TEMPLARS HAD LITTLE OR NO INVOLVEMENT. HOWEVER, THEY WERE HEAVILY INVOLVED WITH THE FIFTH CRUSADE FROM THE START. THREE SUBSEQUENT CRUSADES ALSO SAW TEMPLAR INVOLVEMENT TO VARIOUS DEGREES.

RIGHT The landing of the Crusaders at Damietta in June 1249. In August 1221, the Crusaders had been forced to return the port to the Egyptians, but in 1249 they arrived with an army of around 15,000 men and retook Damietta within days.

A Fifth Crusade fund was set up at the Paris Temple in 1217, and the Templars, joining forces with the other military orders, captured Damietta in June 1218. The Templars as usual rose to the challenge, using both a fleet of ships and pontoons to fight in the waterlogged Nile Delta. They also negotiated the swamps on horseback – an entirely different terrain to the arid environment that most Crusades were fought in. The capture of Damietta put the Crusaders in a strong bargaining position and the Egyptian sultan, al-Kamil, offered them Jerusalem in return for Damietta. The Crusaders accepted, but believing that Jerusalem could not be held on its own, called for reinforcements, which

never arrived. Alone, they attempted to attack Cairo, but failed to guard their flanks. The Egyptians retained control of the water reservoirs along the River Nile and opened the sluice gates, creating floods that trapped the whole crusading army who were then forced to surrender Damietta to the Egyptians.

The Sixth Crusade in 1227 saw diplomacy triumph over warfare. After peaceful negotiations, Jerusalem was returned to Christian hands, with whom it remained for 15 years. Yet the arbitration gave rise to accusations of treachery and caused even more unrest among the inhabitants of Outremer. There followed two more Crusades, the Seventh,

RIGHT Thirteenth-century illustration of the taking of Damietta during the Fifth Crusade. In spring 1218 the Crusaders began their siege of Damietta, and despite resistance from the unprepared Sultan al-Kamil, captured the city that summer, putting the Crusaders in a strong bargaining position.

causing similar capturing and surrendering of regions and cities, and the Eighth. However, neither of these helped the forces in Outremer; the numbers involved were too small, the duration too short and the interests of the participants too diverse to achieve anything worthwhile.

THE MAMLUKS AND THE MONGOLS

The destruction of the remaining Crusader territories gathered pace as two new powers rose to threaten them – the Mongols from inner Asia and the Mamluks, who were slave soldiers from non-Muslim families in Turkey, Eastern Europe and the Caucasus. Because the Mongols were an immediate threat, the Templars, the Hospitallers and the Teutonic Order forgot their disagreements of recent years and put on a united front against them. Then in 1260, the Mamluks annihilated the Mongols. Next, they decided to eliminate the Christians. They began attacking Christian territories as early as 1261. Using the slow method of siege warfare, they eventually captured the Christian towns of Caesarea, Jaffa

and Antioch, leading to the Eighth Crusade in 1270. Again using negotiation rather than warfare, Prince Edward of England persuaded the Mamluks to agree to a ten-year truce in 1272 then returned to England to become Edward I.

THE FALL OF ACRE

Ten years later, negotiations were made for another truce, but the Mamluks broke their word. On 5 April 1291, they began their siege of Acre and broke through on 25 May. They were beaten back by the Templars, but that night, the Templar commander, Theobald Gaudin, sailed from Acre to Sidon with Templar treasure and as many Christian women and children as he could rescue. Three days later, the Temple at Acre fell, all knights fighting to the death.

ABOVE St Francis of Assisi (1181–1226) meeting Sultan al-Kamil at Damietta in 1219 during the Fifth Crusade. The monk went to the Holy Land to preach to the Muslims. He was allowed through the enemy lines to meet the Sultan, who told him that Muslims were as firmly convinced of the truth of Islam as Francis was of the truth of Christianity.

LEFT Eleventh-century miniature painting of a Mongol chief with bow and arrows. The Mongols' success relied on their proficiency at archery and travelling light. They had a remarkable ability to co-ordinate armies separated by great distances and they were ruthless in battle.

THE WEAKENING ORDER

BY MID-AUGUST 1291, THE LAST REMAINING TEMPLAR STRONGHOLDS IN OUTREMER WERE TAKEN BY THE MAMLUKS. IRONICALLY, THE TEMPLARS WERE THE LAST TO GIVE UP THE FIGHT FOR THE HOLY LAND, BUT THEY WERE SUBSEQUENTLY BLAMED FOR ITS LOSS. IN THE AFTERMATH OF THEIR DEFEAT AT ACRE, THE ORDER'S FUNDAMENTAL CAUSE WAS TO CONTINUE TO HELP PILGRIMS AND ULTIMATELY, TO REGAIN CONTROL OF THE HOLY LAND. THE PUBLIC STILL BELIEVED IN THE KNIGHTS TEMPLAR, BUT QUESTIONS BEGAN TO BE RAISED ABOUT THE MILITARY ORDERS, THEIR RESPONSIBILITIES AND FAILURES, THEIR RIVALRIES AND THEIR ARROGANCE.

BELOW Jacques de Molay who continued to lead the Templars from their headquarters in Limassol, Cyprus, from 1293, aiming to regain land in Outremer as soon as possible.

The Templars continued to defend the surviving Christian states of Armenia and Cyprus; helping refugees to escape from the Holy Land and supporting the other military orders, which had been greatly affected by their losses. They continued to build reserves with their business enterprises and donations and carried on with their charitable commitments.

Every religious order had charitable obligations that varied depending on that order's vocation. Then Pope Nicholas IV stated publicly that the rivalry that had arisen between the Templars and the Hospitallers, through the latter imitating Templars' military activities, had contributed to the downfall of Acre and declared that the two orders should be merged. This was not well received by the Templars or the Hospitallers, who resented being made scapegoats for the loss of land in Palestine.

ABOVE Pope Boniface VIII, 1235–1303, who granted the Knights Templar the same rights in Cyprus as they had benefited from in Outremer.

RIGHT Pope Nicholas IV, 1288–92, was stirred by the loss of Acre in 1291 to renewed enthusiasm for a crusade. He declared that the military orders' quarrels had been a contributory factor in the defeat and he suggested that the Templars and the Hospitallers should be amalgamated. Neither Order wanted to give up their independence and resented being punished for the errors of others.

HOLDING ON TO PAPAL APPROVAL

Theobald Gaudin was elected Grand Master after the fall of Acre, but did not live long. By 1293, a new Grand Master had been elected at the Order's new headquarters at Limassol in Cyprus. Jacques de Molay had joined the Order in 1265, when he was about 20 years old. He was straightforward and unimaginative and he believed that the Templars should try to regain land in Outremer as soon as possible. In 1294, he travelled to Europe to gather support and arrived in Rome just as the new Pope, Boniface VIII, was being invested. Boniface granted them the same privileges in Cyprus as they had in Outremer. Molay was in contact with all the European monarchs and from Rome he travelled around Italy, then to Paris and London.

PLANS TO ATTACK

Charles II of Naples allowed the Templars exports of food from south Italian ports free from taxes. Edward I promised to provide a crusading army and exempted the Order from paying export taxes on funds that passed from the London Temple to Cyprus. Other benefits followed.

Negotiations began with the Mongols for a combined attack to reclaim the Holy Land. The Templars began to plan a series of raids to be carried out during the summer of 1300 on the cities of Egypt and Syria. In November, Templar knights went to Ruad to prepare for an invasion of the mainland and waited for their allies. Three months later, in February 1301, Mongol and Armenian allies arrived, but the Templars had given up waiting and had returned to Cyprus.

ENTREPRENEURIAL SKILLS

Despite the failures in the Holy Land, the Templars continued to develop their financial and entrepreneurial expertise, improving their progressive banking, farming and building methods. They had their own sea ports and shipyards, their own hospitals and doctors and their own skills in the use of medicine. An example of their forward thinking is the fact that they accepted epilepsy as a treatable illness – a view that was not held by the rest of Christendom.

ABOVE The Templars and Hospitallers were the closest of all the Orders. If Templars lost sight of their banner in battle, they would immediately look to join the Hospitallers. However, disputes between the Orders were renowned. Occasionally this rivalry broke out into open conflict and it was this negative side of their relationship that outsiders focused on.

THE KING AND THE POPE

PHILIP IV WAS BORN IN THE YEAR 1268, 150 YEARS AFTER THE FORMATION OF THE KNIGHTS TEMPLAR, AND WAS KING OF FRANCE FROM 1285 TO 1314. HE WAS COLD AND SECRETIVE AND WANTED TO MAKE FRANCE MORE IMPORTANT AND POWERFUL. IN ORDER TO ACCOMPLISH THIS PLAN, HE NEEDED LARGE FINANCIAL RESOURCES AND A WEAK POPE. HE PLANNED TO UNITE ALL THE MILITARY ORDERS, AND TAKE ULTIMATE CONTROL OVER THEM. NATURALLY, JACQUES DE MOLAY, GRAND MASTER AT THE TIME, WAS NOT IN FAVOUR OF THIS, AS NONE OF THE OTHER ORDERS WERE AS DISCIPLINED AS THE TEMPLARS.

In his quest for more money, Philip recalled all French coinage and melted it down for his own use. He then replaced it all with coins minted of lesser value. By devaluing the French currency in this way, he was forced to seek refuge in the Paris Temple from an angry mob. The Temple, a strong building that doubled as a kind of bank, served as the Templar headquarters in Paris, although the main headquarters were by then in Cyprus. Philip would have been particularly humiliated, as he had applied to join the Order when he was younger and had suffered the indignity of being rejected. It was also probably here that he became aware of the true wealth of the Knights Templar, and while under their protection, he first contemplated the idea of stealing their vast wealth for his own political agenda.

THE UNLIKELY POPE

Pope Clement V was originally the Archbishop of Bordeaux and was actually a subject of King Edward I of England, but from his youth he had been a personal friend of Philip IV.

LEFT Fifteenth-century drawing of Pope Clement V, whose allegiance was with France rather than Rome. His election was possibly a step towards impartiality, but it backfired. He was suspected by many outside France and England as a puppet of the King of France.

LEFT Edward I (1239–1307), King of England, seated with bishops and monks. In 1294, Edward had promised De Molay he would provide a crusading army to help the Templars once he had dealt with the French and the Scots. This never happened, as he died in July 1307.

LEFT Engraving of Philip IV of France, who was determined to strengthen the French monarchy at any cost. He levied taxes on the French clergy of one half their annual incomes, causing an uproar within the Roman Catholic Church and the papacy, prompting Pope Boniface VIII to issue the bull *Clericis Laicos,* forbidding the transference of any Church property to the French Crown. His rule later initiated the decline of the papacy's totalitarian regime.

He came from a distinguished family, but his elevation to Pope was not, in fact, due to his influential background; Philip IV chose him because he thought Clement would be amenable to his bidding and Edward I chose him because he was the son of one of Edward's vassals. Clement settled in Avignon in France, and throughout his time in office, never set foot in Rome. In his first year as pontiff, Clement appointed ten new cardinals, nine from France and one from England. Indebted as he was to Philip's influence over his election, he could hardly refuse the King's demands. The main demand, of course, was the suppression of the Order of the Poor Knights of the Temple of Solomon.

THE THREAT OF DESTRUCTION

Clement believed passionately in the idea of recapturing the Holy Land for Christianity. He also thought that a crusade would only succeed if it were led by the King of France. Philip liked the idea, and believed that if he were the head of the united military orders, nothing would stop him or his sons after him. A Norman lawyer, Pierre Dubois, a propagandist for the French government, proposed a plan for this French-led crusade. Central to his theme was the amalgamation of the Templars and the Hospitallers

and the control of their resources by Philip IV. Ominously, at the end, Dubois added that it might be necessary "to destroy the Order of the Templars completely, and for the needs of justice, to annihilate it totally".[3]

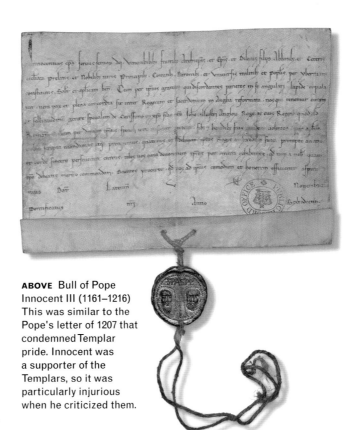

ABOVE Bull of Pope Innocent III (1161–1216) This was similar to the Pope's letter of 1207 that condemned Templar pride. Innocent was a supporter of the Templars, so it was particularly injurious when he criticized them.

ENEMIES WITHIN

FOR NEARLY 200 YEARS, THE POOR KNIGHTS OF THE ORDER OF THE TEMPLE OF SOLOMON WERE THE EMBODIMENT OF CHRISTIANITY'S CRUSADE AGAINST ISLAM. THEY HAD MAINTAINED A STANDING ARMY AND HAD BUILT OR REINFORCED FORTIFICATIONS THROUGHOUT OUTREMER. THEY NOW REALIZED THAT HOLDING ON TO THE HOLY LAND WAS AN IMPRACTICAL IDEA, DISSOLVING A SIGNIFICANT PART OF THEIR ORIGINAL *RAISON D'ÊTRE*. IN ESSENCE, THEY HAD FAILED. YET, IN ALL THEIR EXISTENCE, WHILE THEY HAD BEEN FIGHTING THE INFIDEL, THEY HAD NEVER REALIZED THAT THEIR MOST DANGEROUS ENEMIES WOULD EMERGE FAR CLOSER TO HOME.

RIGHT James II, King of Aragon. In October 1307, he received a letter from Philip IV of France, advising him to seize the Templars' property.

Without the Holy Land, the Templars were more vulnerable than ever. Resentment against them was mounting in some areas. Some questioned their culture of secrecy; their initiation rites were always conducted clandestinely and they often acted as secret messengers for popes and kings, as Templars were rarely challenged. Others were antagonized by their vast wealth. Although still respected and revered by most, their success in commercial and economic activities aroused a degree of envy. Some questioned why, now they had no official role, they were still awarded so many privileges. Yet, this rancour was unlikely to progress any further. As an Order of the Catholic Church,

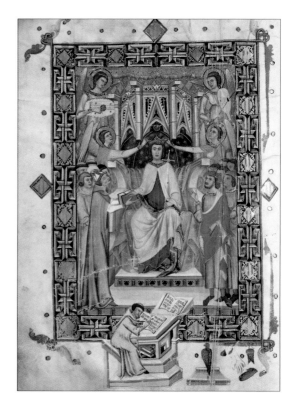

RIGHT Early fourteenth-century fresco of Philip IV (1268–1314), King of France from 1285. He was exceptionally pious, a skilled hunter and an accomplished knight and he was deeply affected by the death of his wife, Joan of Navarre, in 1305. As the Templars were only accountable to the Pope, the only way that Philip could lawfully seize their assets was to accuse them of magic and heresy.

any move against the Knights Templar was a direct assault against the papacy itself. The Pope, however, was able to cast aspersions.

In 1303, King Philip IV of France sent a force of French soldiers to kidnap Pope Boniface VIII in order to put him on trial in France on charges of heresy, sodomy and the murder of the previous pope, Celestine V. The nominal force of Templars and Hospitallers guarding him prevented his capture, but the shock of the attempt killed him within a month.

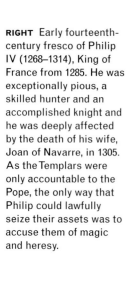

THE ALLEGATIONS

To be expelled from the Order was the highest punishment a Templar knight could face. Upon expulsion, he had an obligation to join the Cistercians, who always had a close relationship with the Templars. It was believed that by joining this non-warrior monastic order, the expelled Templar would save his soul. Some knights who had been expelled from the Order – Esquin of Floyan, the prior of Montfaucon, Bernard Pelet, prior of the Mas-d'Agenais, and a knight from Gisors, Gérard of Byzol – went to King James II of Aragon with accusations against the Templars. James was unconvinced, so they went to Philip of France with their allegations of gross impropriety.

After the investiture of Pope Clement V in 1305, the idea of merging the Templars with the Hospitallers returned. Jacques de Molay and Fulk de Villaret, Grand Master of the Hospitallers, were summoned to a meeting with the new Pope at Poitiers. While there, Jacques de Molay raised the matter of certain charges that had been made against members of the Temple. Whether they were believed or doubted, he asked the Pope to initiate an enquiry to re-establish any uncertainty over the Order's reputation. In August 1307, Clement wrote to Philip, saying he was greatly saddened and could scarcely believe it, but he wanted to make further enquiries into the matter.

ABOVE Pope Boniface VIII quarrelled with Philip IV and excommunicated him in 1303. Within days, Philip's soldiers burst into the papal palace to arrest him.

LEFT Philip IV the Fair became King of France at the age of 17, inheriting his father's debts which he calculated would take over 300 years to repay. At the same time, his war with England had to be paid for.

THE ARRESTS

CLEMENT V ASKED PHILIP TO WAIT UNTIL HE RECOVERED FROM AN INCAPACITATING ILLNESS BEFORE THEY INVESTIGATED THE TEMPLARS. PHILIP IGNORED THE REQUEST AND ON FRIDAY, 13 OCTOBER 1307, IN SURPRISE DAWN RAIDS, HIS AGENTS ARRESTED 5,000 TEMPLARS IN FRANCE, INCLUDING JACQUES DE MOLAY, WHO WAS SEIZED AT THE PARIS TEMPLE, ON THE CHARGES OF HERESY, SODOMY, BLASPHEMY AND DENYING CHRIST. SINCE THAT DATE, FRIDAY THE 13TH HAS BEEN CONSIDERED VERY UNLUCKY.

RIGHT Illuminated letter c.1350, showing a fool denying the existence of God. At the time it was accepted that no thinking person would renounce God, thus the Templars must have been fools.

BELOW This fourteenth-century illustration shows arrested Templars brought before Pope Clement V and King Philip IV where, once the threat of torture was lifted, they protested their innocence.

Philip's actions caused incredulity among the crowned heads of Europe and shook Western Europe to the core. The Italians, writing at the time, were quite convinced that Philip had fabricated the charges for his own financial motives and the new Edward II of England said that he could not believe it. Most European powers believed it was Philip's jealousy, along with greed and a nearly bankrupt nation, that prompted him to make the arrests. Indeed, as with the Jews and the Lombards, Philip confiscated all that his men

could find of the Templars' property and wealth. Mysteriously, his men found virtually nothing. Even Clement was enraged by this because the Templars were a religious and humble Christian order.

INQUISITION

After being arrested, the Templars were placed in solitary confinement for varying lengths of time, from a few days to years. They were brought before the Inquisition individually and without any legal representation. The accusations against them were read to them and they were then told that an admission of the charges would secure their pardon and liberty, but refusal to do this would be followed by the death penalty. When the desired evidence had been secured, the witness was asked to state that his testimony had been given voluntarily, then it was written down by two clerks. Some Templars were put on the rack three or four times before the Inquisition could extract the desired answer.

LEFT *The Supplication of the Heretics*, c.1450 by Fouquet. This fifteenth-century painting shows the fate of heretics – or of those accused of heresy, whether innocent or guilty – in the Middle Ages. It was thought at that time that burning cleansed the soul, which was an important consideration for those convicted of heresy.

ABOVE Engraving of King Edward II of England. He found the charges made against the Templars implausible and wrote to the kings of France, Aragon, Portugal, Naples and Castile to say so.

LEFT Illustration from a thirteenth-century manuscript of heretics burning theological books. Philip IV and Clement V accused the Templars of atheism, sodomy, blasphemy and more. In the Middle Ages, these accusations inspired suspicion and fear among everyone.

On 25 October, Jacques de Molay confessed before an assembly from the University of Paris that he denied Christ and spat on the Cross. Other confessions followed from all other senior Templars in captivity. Philip once more urged the other sovereigns of Europe to arrest Templars in their countries. On 22 November 1307, Pope Clement tried to take over the proceedings and ordered the arrests of Templars throughout Christendom in order to extract the truth. Arrests were eventually made in all countries, but as torture was prohibited in several countries, not all arrests solicited confessions. There was widespread disbelief of the Templars' genuine guilt outside France.

Templars' confessions varied, depending on the intensity of torture used. Most confessed to spitting, trampling and urinating on the Cross in their initiation ceremonies and denying Christ as a false prophet. Many confessed to worshipping spurious deities. There were also confessions of killing newborn babies.

In the fourteenth century, heresy and magic elicited genuine terror. To the people of Europe, the blasphemous confessions were profoundly shocking, but they were not aware of how the confessions had been extracted.

CHARGES AGAINST THE TEMPLARS

The charges that Philip IV of France brought against the Templars were based on myths about heresy and magic. Many were misinterpretations of the Order's legitimate practices. The charges included: obscene kisses at their initiation; veneration of false idols; not making charitable gifts; not believing in the Mass or other sacraments of the Church; and being in league with the Devil.

THE TRIALS

IN ACCORDANCE WITH THE RULE OF THE ORDER, LITERACY AND EDUCATION WERE DISCOURAGED.
SO ALTHOUGH JACQUES DE MOLAY WAS AN EARNEST AND RELIGIOUS MAN WHO ATTENDED MASS
FAITHFULLY, HE WAS ILLITERATE AND UNLEARNED IN THEOLOGY. IT WAS THIS IGNORANCE THAT
ENABLED HIS INQUISITORS TO TRIUMPH OVER HIM AND OTHER TEMPLARS DURING THEIR TRIALS.

RIGHT An engraving of
Jacques de Molay, the
elderly and earnest last
Templar. According to
one account, he opened
his shirt when he met
Clement V a month after
his arrest, in order to
display the marks of
torture on his body.

BELOW The Templars,
when not being tortured,
maintained that they
were faithful Catholics
and upheld the Rule that
St Bernard had given the
Order in 1127.

Pope Clement V insisted that the Templars'
confessions should be heard before a papal
committee and on 24 December, Jacques de
Molay and other senior Templars appeared before
it. When De Molay and the other Templars were
away from Philip's torturers, they retracted their
statements on the grounds that they had only
confessed after being tortured. In February 1308,
Clement suspended proceedings. Philip appealed
to doctors at the University of Paris, but they
told him he did not have a case.

HOUSE ARREST AND HEARINGS

In June 1308, Clement arrived in Poitiers to try
to sort out the affair. Philip put him under virtual
house arrest with soldiers sealing off the town.
Clement, trapped, was aware of Philip's behaviour
towards Pope Boniface, and was fearful of his own
position. In August, he agreed to split the
convictions with the King and share the prosecution
of the Templars. The Pope's men would judge
individuals of the Order and the King's men would
judge the Order as an entity. He issued the bull
Fasciens misericordiam, which set out the prosecution
process, and proceedings commenced. A council at
Vienne was to decide the future of the Order of the
Temple, while the Temple dignitaries, among them
Jacques de Molay, were to be judged by the Pope.

RIGHT Pope Clement V presiding over the council of Vienne in 1311, where the complaint against the Templars was the first and greatest concern. The council began on 16 October 1311 in the presence of 20 cardinals, 4 patriarchs, about 100 archbishops and bishops, and several abbots and priors.

In the royal palace at Chinon, Jacques de Molay was again questioned by the Pope's men, but this time with agents of King Philip in attendance. Once more, he declared his guilt and was taken back to prison, and left there for a year. In November 1309, the Papal Commission for the Kingdom of France began its hearings. When De Molay gave evidence on 26 November, he said that he wanted to defend the Order because it was incredible that the Church should want to destroy it, but he doubted his ability to do so without help. He realized that illiteracy was his biggest problem. Within the Order were some of the best bankers, farmers, knights and masons, for instance, but not one lawyer. This was directly in line with St Bernard's Rule.

After two years of torture and imprisonment, it was De Molay's ignorance that prevented him from mounting a defence and it allowed his enemies to gain an advantage over him and the rest of the Order. He admitted that he did not have the ability to defend his Order as he was but a poor, unlettered knight and that the Pope had to decide the case.

DE MOLAY'S DEFENCE

In his defence, De Molay had only three things to say. The first was that the liturgies in Templar churches were more beautiful than in any other churches, other than cathedrals. The second was that the Order had been generous in its charitable donations, and the third was that no other Order "had shed its blood so readily in defence of the Christian faith".[4]

LEFT Christ leading the Crusaders into battle, from a manuscript of the late Middle Ages, showing the propaganda that tried to encourage people to join the fight in the Holy Land. The Templars had been revered as soldiers of Christ but were now being condemned with seemingly little reason.

On two occasions, De Molay unequivocally stated that he did not acknowledge accusations brought against his Order. He trusted that the Pope would triumph over the will of the King.

THE END OF THE ORDER

THE COMMISSION WAS SUSPENDED UNTIL 1310, WHEN A FULL LIST OF THE 127 CHARGES MADE AGAINST THE ORDER WAS READ OUT. BY NOW, MANY OF THE INCARCERATED TEMPLARS WERE AFRAID THAT THEIR IMPRISONMENT WOULD BE MADE WORSE OR THAT THEY WOULD BE BULLIED OR TORTURED IN OTHER WAYS IF THEY CONTINUED TO TRY TO DEFEND THE ORDER. AT PARIS, RHEIMS AND SENS, 133 TEMPLARS DIED FROM TORTURE BECAUSE THEY WOULD NOT PERJURE THEMSELVES AND INCRIMINATE THEIR ORDER. THE CHARGES WERE CAREFULLY CONSTRUCTED TO TRAP THE UNLEARNED MEN OF THE ORDER.

RIGHT Philip IV attending the execution of Jacques de Molay and Geoffrey de Charney on 18 March 1314.

BELOW Jacques de Molay and Geoffrey de Charney sentenced to the stake in 1314, from the Chronicle of France, written by the monks of St Denis.

Over 600 Templars came forward to defend the Order, but as most had previously confessed to the charges which they were now denying, they were considered by law to be relapsed heretics. The punishment for this was burning at the stake. On 12 May 1310, 54 Templars burned at the stake, professing their innocence. Trials of the rest of the Order continued for another four years.

COLLAPSE OF THE TEMPLAR DEFENCE

One of the admissions that the Templars made during their trials was that they had been friendly with the sultan and the Saracens in Outremer, otherwise it would have been impossible for them to survive there. To their judges, this was highly suspicious. How could men of the Church fraternize with the enemy? If they were friends with Saracens, this meant that at least some of the Templars spoke Arabic. The best use for Arabic, many believed, was for reading magic texts. In this and many other allegations, the questioners took advantage of the Templars' ignorance of theology and confused them.

THE FINAL JUDGEMENT

On 18 March 1314, De Molay and three other
chief officers of the Order were led to a platform
in front of Notre Dame, where their sentences
were read out. As guilty of heresy, they were
told, they were to be condemned to harsh and
perpetual imprisonment. After seven years in
prison, the last four in solitary confinement, this
was perhaps too much for De Molay. Now over
70, he had trusted that the Pope would declare
their innocence in the end. He shouted that he
and his Order were innocent of all crimes and
he publicly withdrew his confession. Geoffrey
de Charney, one of the Order's Commanders
and in his 60s, joined De Molay in renouncing
their earlier confessions. As with the other
Templars who had previously been burned at the
stake, once they retracted their confession for
heresy, this made them relapsed heretics and the
only punishment for that was death by fire.
Philip was told at once. That evening, Jacques
de Molay and Geoffrey de Charney were taken
to a small island in the River Seine to be burned
at the stake.

In front of a crowd, De Molay asked to be tied
facing Notre Dame so that he could die in prayer.
As the flames licked higher, De Molay protested
the innocence of the Order once more and he
invited both Clement and Philip to join him
within the year.

It is generally agreed that the reason
for Philip's actions was envy of the Templars'
wealth and seemingly limitless power, as well as
his humiliation at being rejected as a Templar
some years before. By destroying them, his debt
to the Templars was wiped out, but he gained
nothing more. Their spectacular fall from grace
shook the world.

ABOVE The interior of
Temple Church, London,
completed in 1185. After
the destruction and
abolition of the Order
in 1307, Edward II took
control of the church as
a Crown possession. It
was later given to the
Knights Hospitallers,
who rented the Temple to
two colleges of lawyers.

LEFT The Chapel of Our
Lady of the Temple, in
Lanleff, Brittany, France,
based on the Church of
the Holy Sepulchre in
Jerusalem. It was built
in the eleventh century
by the Templars, but is
one of many buildings
left to deteriorate after
their demise.

PART FIVE

SHROUDED IN MYSTERY

King Philip had tried to influence other Christian monarchs, endeavouring to ensure that no Templar anywhere would be spared. He was not completely successful. On 12 October 1307, many Templars escaped before the arrests the next day. After 1312, there were still thousands of Templars left, as most other countries were reluctant to prosecute them. But the Order had been shattered at its core and it never again rose to the power and success it had once held. Since that time, the allegations of the trial have naturally been questioned. The Order's beginnings, zenith and ruin have been discussed and studied, and much of it has become cloaked in mystery. With no official records remaining, the warrior monks disappeared from history into myth, their true nature forgotten and woven into fantasy – which has not diminished over time.

RIGHT Rosslyn Chapel, a fifteenth-century church in Roslin, Scotland. Due to its alleged connections with the Knights Templar, the Chapel has inevitably become part of modern lore as a possible final resting place of the Holy Grail.

WERE THEY HERETICS?

THE ORDER ALWAYS ACCEPTED EXCOMMUNICANTS IN ITS RANKS. WHILE THIS MAY BE SEEN AS BROAD-MINDED AND TOLERANT TO IMPARTIAL HISTORIANS, TO SOME CONTEMPORARY OBSERVERS, IT COULD HAVE BEEN HIGHLY SUSPICIOUS. THE FACT THAT THE TEMPLARS TOLERATED MANY WHO DID NOT ADHERE TO ORTHODOX CATHOLIC BELIEFS CAUSED OTHERS TO QUESTION THEIR LOYALTIES. THEY WERE ALSO SAID TO HAVE FRATERNIZED WITH MUSLIMS AND TO HAVE MADE CONTACT WITH HERETICAL SECTS IN PALESTINE. THEIR APPLICATION OF IDEAS TAKEN FROM ARABIC CULTURE INFLAMED MANY. IN FRANCE, THEY WERE SAID TO HAVE SHELTERED CATHARS AND WITCHES FROM THE AUTHORITIES AND SOME OF THE CHARGES AGAINST THEM WERE THE SAME AS ACCUSATIONS AGAINST WITCHES. THESE MAY HAVE BEEN STANDARD ALLEGATIONS USED BY THOSE WANTING A HERESY CHARGE TO STICK.

RIGHT Pope Innocent III (1198–1216), arguably the most powerful pope in history. He was a vigorous opponent of heresy and proclaimed a crusade against the Albigensians (Cathars).

BELOW A fourteenth-century depiction of the worship of pagan idols. Christians of the Middle Ages made a clear distinction between worshipping religious relics and worshipping pagan idols and this was often confused by the Inquisition.

The unorthodox Cathars, with whom the Order was associated, were also known as Albigensians (or Palatines in Italy). They came from Languedoc in France and parts of northern Italy. They did not have a single definitive church, but consisted of several different factions. They believed in reincarnation and rejected the orthodox Catholic Church, which branded them either as non-Christian or as a heretical Christian sect. Pope Innocent III proclaimed a crusade against them, and from 1208 to 1244, the "Albigensian Crusade" eradicated them.

Bertrand de Blanchefort, the sixth Grand Master, from 1156 to 1169, was supposedly from a Cathar family, and from his time on, the Order welcomed Cathars into its ranks. It had always welcomed excommunicants as it was hard to recruit enough men needed for the force in the Holy Land. This did not explain, however, why the Order had so many Cathars in France, which gave rise to further suspicion that the Templars had been contaminated by the heresy of Catharism.

DEVIL WORSHIP

Anxiety about heresy in general increased dramatically from the eleventh century onward. Many pious people were accused of heresy as one mark of all heretics was their strong conviction about their beliefs. Because of this, several religious Orders were accused of heresy.

LEFT The Battle of Muret during the Albigensian Crusade in 1213. Simon de Montfort was the leader of this crusade (1209–29), which aimed to destroy the Cathars under Raymond of Toulouse.

Charges against the Templars also confirmed medieval beliefs about magicians. Certain texts written by ancient philosophers, prophets and scientists claimed to show how, through knowledge of the heavens and the Earth, it was possible to control events according to one's will. Reading these books was seen as devil-worship.

Necromancy, a method to raise the spirit of the dead, was particularly popular, but books written on the subject emphasized the importance of secrecy, to keep the books away from the eyes of the uninitiated. The charges against the Templars implied that the Order's Rule might be such a book. Charges also hinted that the Arabic texts that some Templars read were possibly magic too. Pope Clement V could have disproved this instantly, as he owned two copies of the Rule and had access to Arabic-speaking people who could have translated any books held by the Order.

SPITTING ON THE CROSS

Interestingly, a charge that the Templars did not deny was that they spat on the Cross and denied Christ. Such sacrilegious practices enabled them to prepare for the sort of torture they might endure at the hands of the Saracens. De Molay explained that they could train themselves to deny their religion "with the mind only, not with the heart".[5]

NO WAY OUT

Once a person had been accused of heresy in the Middle Ages, they could not refute the charge unless they could show that the person who had brought the charge was a personal enemy. It was difficult to find someone to speak on the accused's behalf as anyone defending a heretic was likely to be charged with heresy too. In 1252, Pope Innocent IV licensed the use of torture in heresy cases. A person who confessed to heresy and repented would be given penance and absolved. A person who was believed to be guilty but who refused to confess was punished by death.

ABOVE A twentieth-century illuminated manuscript from Languedoc, showing the capture of Montségur Castle, France, where over 200 Cathars were burned alive during the thirteenth-century Albigensian Crusade. In March 1244, 10,000 French Catholic troops set fire to the castle, turning the Cathar defenders into a human bonfire.

VISITING THE NEW WORLD

MANY OF THE TEMPLARS AVOIDED ARREST. SOME ESCAPED TO VARIOUS PARTS OF EUROPE, INCLUDING PORTUGAL, WHERE THEY RENAMED THEMSELVES THE KNIGHTS OF CHRIST. OTHERS POSSIBLY FLED TO SCOTLAND WERE THEY WERE WELCOMED BY THE SCOTTISH KING, ROBERT THE BRUCE. SEVERAL TEMPLARS APPEAR TO HAVE FOUGHT WITH ROBERT THE BRUCE AT BANNOCKBURN IN 1312 AND PLAYED A KEY ROLE IN OVERWHELMING THE ENGLISH ARMY. ANOTHER THEORY LINKING SCOTLAND WITH THE TEMPLARS CONCERNS THE DISCOVERY OF AMERICA. IT IS CALLED "LA MERIKA THEORY" AFTER THE STAR SYMBOL "MERICA" USED ON TEMPLAR SHIPS AND IN BATTLE. LA MERIKA IS BELIEVED TO HAVE BEEN TAKEN FROM THE NAME OF THE FIVE-POINTED STAR OF ISHTAR, THE BABYLONIAN GODDESS.

RIGHT Amerigo Vespucci (1454–1512), Italian explorer and geographer who died saying that he did not make the voyage to the "New World" after all. Scholars still question whether he reached America at all.

BELOW America; an allegorical frontispiece with medallion portraits of the Portuguese explorer, Christopher Columbus (1451–1506) and Amerigo Vespucci on either side of a globe showing the Americas.

It is claimed that the Templars travelled to America long before either Christopher Columbus or Amerigo Vespucci. History has often stated that in 1492 Christopher Columbus discovered America, although we know that Vikings were probably there centuries before. In 1497, it is said that Amerigo Vespucci made a voyage looking for the "New World". On his return, in 1504, he described the new world he saw and soon the name "America" first appeared on a map and globe created by a German cartographer, thought to be named after Vespucci. However, some historians point out that countries' and continents'

names are normally based on surnames, not first names. Furthermore, even though Vespucci described the New World on his return, on his deathbed he denied making any such discovery.

SEAFARING CAPABILITIES

The harbour of La Rochelle on the Atlantic coast was designed and developed by the Templars early in their history and became their most important harbour. They owned a vast fleet and other seaports in France, yet La Rochelle was the most important Templar province. One theory claims that the Templars travelled from La Rochelle

to Canada and America. After their demise, it has been suggested that some Templars sailed to America and Canada again from Scotland. Some say it was to hide or safeguard treasure. Whatever the truth in this, the Templars had the fleet and the seafaring credentials to undertake such voyages.

Sir Henry Sinclair of Rosslyn, a trusted friend of Robert the Bruce who had fought at Bannockburn with him, wanted to explore the North Atlantic Sea. Descended from the Vikings, Sinclair intended to follow the paths they had laid down. Sir Henry also had many links with the Templars. The Templar preceptory in Scotland was in the vicinity of the Scottish Sinclairs and Henry Sinclair's ancestor was Henri de Saint-Clair who was with Godfroi de Bouillon when Jerusalem was taken from the Saracens. In addition, several Sinclairs and Saint-Clairs had been Templars. Two Venetian sailors, the Zeno brothers, captained two of Sinclair's ships and they set sail from Scotland in 1397 with a fleet of 13 further ships.

In 1558, a descendant of Zeno's published a manuscript and an extremely accurate map of the North Atlantic voyage, although neither Sinclair nor the Templars were mentioned.

THE NEW COUNTRY

It is thought that Sinclair and the Templars reached Nova Scotia (Latin for New Scotland), Canada, in 1398 and moved south to New England about a year later. Several old gravestones in Nova Scotia are marked with Crusader Crosses and near the summit of Prospect Hill in Westford, Massachusetts, is a hand-chiselled gravestone in the style of the Templars. The image on the stone is of a Templar, Sir James Gunn, who was a member of Sinclair's expedition.

In 1440, Sir William Sinclair, Sir Henry's grandson, began building the Rosslyn Chapel in Scotland. In the chapel are stone carvings of American plants, such as aloe vera, supposedly not seen by Europeans until Columbus returned. The chapel was completed in 1486 yet Columbus did not make his first voyage until 1492.

ABOVE Interior of Rosslyn Chapel showing the Apprentice's Pillar. The interior of Rosslyn Chapel was vastly expensive to build and displays many mysterious and elaborate stone carvings, some of which are of American plants not known in Britain at the time.

LEFT Representation of the Templar port of La Rochelle, 1736. In the twelfth century, the Duke of Aquitaine granted the port the right to become a commune, and, thanks to the profileration of trade this encouraged, La Rochelle became the largest French harbour on the coast of the Atlantic until the fifteenth century. It would have been from here that the Templars embarked on their theoretical voyage to what is now Canada.

TEMPLE MOUNT TREASURE

KING BALDWIN II OF JERUSALEM HAD ALLOWED THE FIRST TEMPLARS TO DO AS THEY PLEASED WITH THE WING HE HAD GIVEN THEM IN THE TEMPLE MOUNT. ONE BELIEF THAT HAS PERSISTED OVER THE CENTURIES IS THAT THEY WERE INVOLVED IN ARCHAEOLOGICAL EXCAVATIONS BENEATH THE TEMPLE PLATFORM IN WHAT IS KNOWN AS SOLOMON'S STABLES. THIS SUSPICION OF CLANDESTINE ACTIVITY INVOLVED THE IDEA THAT THE TEMPLARS HAD SOMETHING TO HIDE — OR TO FIND — UNDER THERE.

RIGHT The Dome of the Rock was built between AD687 and AD691 by Byzantine craftsmen under the 9th Caliph, Abd al-Malik. Located in what Muslims call the Noble Sanctuary (*Haram al-Sharif*) and what Jews and Christians call the Temple Mount, it remains one of Jerusalem's best-known landmarks.

BELOW Map showing the old city of Jerusalem during the Crusader period.

In AD70, the Second Temple, which then stood in place of Solomon's Temple, was sacked by Roman legions under Titus. The supposition is that something exceptionally important was left there, overlooked because of its highly concealed location. Conjecture as to whether Hugues de Payens and the Count of Champagne knew about this when they went to Jerusalem has continued for centuries. It would give reason for the Count's visits to the Holy Land before the Order was officially formed, explain why he wanted to join

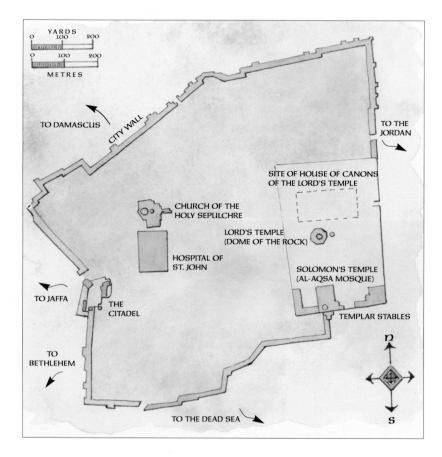

> ### SACRED SITE
> Temple Mount is one of the most contested religious sites in the world. It is believed to be where God gathered earth to create Adam; where Cain, Abel and Noah offered sacrifices to God; and where Jacob slept when he dreamt of angels. It is where Abraham nearly sacrificed his son to God and where Mohammed briefly passed on a winged steed, Buraq, on his way to visit Heaven with the Archangel Gabriel. It is alleged that the Ark of the Covenant was housed there.

"La Milice du Christ", why he accepted his former vassal as his Grand Master and why Hugues de Payens went to Baldwin II at the Temple Mount in the first place. It has been considered that the reason there were only nine Templars during their first decade was because their mission of excavation beneath the Temple Mount was top secret.

LEFT Illustration from a Mozarabic Bible of the Carrying of the Ark of the Covenant. Mozarabs were Spanish Christians living under Muslim rule during the sixth to eleventh centuries.

BELOW Interior of the Dome of the Rock, Temple Mount. The walls are covered in Islamic art, mosaics, marble and faience. The columns are built with the finest marble and the arches richly decorated with mosaics, painted plaster and jewels.

On the other hand, the digging could have been because they were fascinated by the principles of "sacred" geometry that the Temple had been designed on. It is feasible that they wanted to learn more about it for their own future building projects.

THE STABLES OF SOLOMON

From 1124, the Templars housed their horses in the Stables of Solomon, which were large enough to hold 2,000 horses. In the 68 years that they occupied the Temple Mount, they certainly undertook a great deal of building work, starting in 1120. This could have been simply with the intention of making the place suitable for a strict order of military monks or it could have been for another reason. Rumours about their findings have continued since the early years of the Templars' foundation, but it has never been established whether they actually found anything – or if they did, what it was.

Suggestions of what they might have found range from the relics of saints, the embalmed head of St John the Baptist or even Jesus himself, to parts of the True Cross, documents about the true origins of Christianity or the Ark of the Covenant. Alternatively, it has been said that it was the treasure of the Second Temple – priceless metals, precious stones and gold – left behind and undetected by the Romans.

THE SKULL OF SIDON

THE SKULL AND CROSSBONES HAVE LONG BEEN USED AS A SYMBOL OF VANITAS OR A *MEMENTO MORI*, LITERALLY REMINDING US OF OUR OWN MORTALITY. WHEN THE SKULL AND CROSSBONES BEGAN TO BE USED IS NOT CLEAR, BUT IT BECAME A FAIRLY COMMON TEMPLAR TOMBSTONE DECORATION. VERSIONS OF THIS IMAGE OF MORTALITY WERE BELIEVED TO FEATURE IN TEMPLAR RITUAL, NOT FOR ANY SINISTER REASON, BUT AS PART OF THEIR BELIEF THAT OUR PHYSICAL BODIES ARE TRANSIENT, WHILE OUR SOULS ARE ETERNAL. IN ONE TEMPLAR STORY A SKULL IS LINKED TO A MACABRE MYTH.

RIGHT A nineteenth-century impression of tombs of the Knights Templar by Sanquirico, *c.*1820–39. This ethereal painting epitomizes the speculation and intrigue that have surrounded the Templars since the fourteenth century.

Because the Templars were monks, any involvement with women was forbidden. Bernard of Clairvaux had made sure that celibacy was an important part of their Rule as it was for the Cistercian monks and other orders. He believed, as did many Christians, that asceticism kept the mind focused on God and a righteous life. Close relationships with others were an impediment to sanctity because they occupied the will, and a

passionate or violent nature could be tamed by an austere life. According to the Gospels, Jesus was not married and all the priests of Rome were celibate. Yet a chilling story involving a clandestine relationship between a Templar and a woman may explain the skull and crossbones story.

LEFT The church at Kilmartin, in Argyle and Bute, Scotland, contains many examples of Templar graves and tomb carvings showing Templar figures. From the Middle Ages *memento mori* began to be put on gravestones, intended to remind people of their own mortality.

MACABRE MYTH

This is one of the less appealing stories about
the Templars and is a somewhat ghoulish fantasy,
but interesting nonetheless. The legend of the
Skull of Sidon tells of the Templar knight who
had a relationship with a young woman who died.
After she was buried, the knight exhumed her
and consummated their relationship, resulting
in a gruesome birth nine months later:

"A great lady of Maraclea was loved by a
Templar, a Lord of Sidon, but she died in her
youth and on the night of her burial, this wicked
lover crept to the grave, dug up her body and
violated it. Then a voice from the void bade him
return in nine months' time, for he would find
a son. He obeyed the injunction and at the
appointed time he opened the grave again and
found a head on the leg bones of the skeleton
(skull and crossbones). The same voice bade him
'guard it well, for it would be the giver of all good
things' and he carried it away with him. It became
his protecting genius, and he was able to defeat
his enemies by merely showing them the magic
head. In due course, it passed to the possession
of the Order".[6]

This story can be traced back to the twelfth
century, but did not originate with the
Templars. By the time of their trials in the
fourteenth century, it became linked with
them and was mentioned repeatedly in the
Inquisition's records. It is not known where
it originated, but it was clearly used to
discredit the Order.

ABOVE This twentieth-
century painting depicts
the end of the piratical
career of Bartholomew
Roberts, killed during an
attack from the British
Royal Naval warship
Swallow. The skull and
crossbones symbol
adopted by pirates, is
used as a warning of
something that is
dangerous or deadly.
The symbol was used
originally by the Templars
as a *memento mori*,
which literally means,
"remember that you are
mortal", or "remember
your death".

LEFT St Bernard of
Clairvaux played a pivotal
role in the Templars'
planning, conduct and
formation. He was
canonized 21 years after
his death in 1174 and his
skull was placed in Troyes
Cathedral – another skull
of particular holy
importance for the Order.
Interestingly, the skull
was taken to Switzerland
for safety during the
French Revolution.

THE HOLY GRAIL

THE HOLY GRAIL IS PROBABLY THE MOST PREVALENT AND ENDURING MYSTERY THAT SURROUNDS THE KNIGHTS TEMPLAR. FOR SO LONG HAVE THEY BEEN ASSOCIATED WITH THIS ENIGMATIC AND ELUSIVE ISSUE THAT AT TIMES IT CAN BE DIFFICULT TO DISASSOCIATE THEM FROM IT. IN CHRISTIAN MYTHOLOGY, THE HOLY GRAIL HAS BEEN DESCRIBED AS BEING THE CUP OR CHALICE THAT JESUS DRANK FROM AT THE LAST SUPPER, AND SOMETIMES AS THE SAME VESSEL THAT CAUGHT HIS BLOOD WHEN HIS SIDE WAS PIERCED ON THE CROSS. IT HAS ALSO BEEN PORTRAYED AS A MAGICAL EGYPTIAN OR BABYLONIAN STONE; A CELTIC CAULDRON ENDOWED WITH PRODUCTIVE POWERS, SOUGHT AVIDLY BY KING ARTHUR; A SECRET BLOODLINE OF CHRIST; OR EVEN A SOURCE OF ENLIGHTENMENT.

ABOVE In Christian mythology, the Holy Grail was the dish, plate or cup used by Jesus at the Last Supper, said to possess miraculous powers.

RIGHT Mary Magdalene kissing Christ's feet, a detail from *Deposition*, 1443, Fra Angelo. Conspiracy theories have questioned whether Mary Magdalene held the secret to the Holy Grail and whether this was one of the Templars' secrets.

Along with the ambiguity of the Grail is the added question of where the Grail is hidden. Most of the speculation about the Templars digging beneath the Temple Mount and their subsequent voyages to various parts of Europe and America revolves around the idea that they found something and hid it before Philip IV could find it. Many have surmised that this was the Grail.

HIDING PLACES

If the Templars were in possession of something as sacred as the Grail, consistent with their Rule, they would have protected it to the death. Conjecture that they buried it on Oak Island in Nova Scotia has attracted many bounty hunters. Although the island's legendary "money-pit" has yielded nothing, the pit's elaborate engineering which means that it floods every time anyone tries to dig in it and the discovery of a stone inscribed with mysterious writing at 90 feet, have convinced many that it contains Templar treasure. Rosslyn Chapel has also been cited as the hiding place for the Grail because of its alleged connections with the Templars after their suppression. It is said that the apprentice who completed the "Apprentice's pillar" left it hollow so the Grail could be contained inside it. Other hiding places include the "Secret Vaults" below the chapel.

In 1546, Mary of Guise (mother of Mary Queen of Scots) wrote to Lord William Sinclair of Rosslyn, referring to "a great secret within Rosslyn". It is not known what she meant. Scanning and excavations have produced nothing and the building will not withstand any more disruption, but unusually, there are many Templar, Christian and Pagan symbols in the chapel – not all of which are understood.

Legend has it that the Grail was seen by pilgrims in the fifth century and it is said that it was in Constantinople in the thirteenth century. There are many other potential Holy Grail sites and new theories emerge frequently.

LEFT Detail from *The Last Supper*, by Leonardo da Vinci, 1498, fresco in the refectory of Santa Maria delle Grazie, Milan. A theory exists that the person to Jesus' left is Mary Magdalene and not the apostle John (as art historians identify the figure).

Over the centuries, many stories have been written about the Templars and the Grail. Some time between 1180 and 1191, an (unfinished) poem called *Perceval, le Conte du Graal* (*Perceval, The Story of the Grail*) was written by Chrétien de Troyes, who claimed he was working from a source book, which is interesting as he was writing this just after Guillaume de Tyre wrote about the Templars. Between about 1197 and 1209, Wolfram von Eschenbach wrote another verse romance, *Parzival*, portraying the Templars as the guardians of the Grail. After the Middle Ages, this interest waned, but in the nineteenth century, writers such as

Scott, Tennyson and artists such as the Pre-Raphaelite brotherhood rekindled the intrigue. In 1882, Richard Wagner's opera *Parsifal* gave new significance to the theme, for the first time connecting the Grail to female fertility. The beliefs and debates persist, but the connection between the Templars and the Grail remains elusive.

ABOVE The ruins of Dinas Bran Castle sit at the top of a high hill in the valley of the River Dee in Llangollen, Wales. The hill is credited as being one of the resting places of the Holy Grail.

ORIGINS OF THE TERM

The word *graal*, as it was spelt originally, is probably an Old French version of the Latin word *gradalis*, meaning a dish brought to the table during a meal. After the first Grail romances had been written, late medieval writers came up with a new idea, that "sangreal" was another name for "Holy Grail". In Old French, *san grial* means "Holy Grail" and *sang rial* means "royal blood".

LEFT A gargoyle in Rosslyn Chapel holding a chalice, which has helped to propagate ideas about the Chapel and the Holy Grail.

THE TURIN SHROUD

ANOTHER PERSISTENT MYSTERY ABOUT THE TEMPLARS CONCERNS THE TURIN SHROUD. THIS IS AN OLD
LINEN CLOTH MEASURING 4.4 X 1.1M (14.4 X 3.6 FT). IMPRINTED ON THE FABRIC IS THE FAINT IMAGE
OF A MAN WHO APPEARS TO HAVE BEEN PHYSICALLY TRAUMATIZED IN A MANNER CONSISTENT WITH
CRUCIFIXION. IT IS KEPT IN THE ROYAL CHAPEL OF THE CATHEDRAL OF ST JOHN THE BAPTIST IN
TURIN, ITALY. BELIEVED BY MANY TO BE THE BURIAL SHROUD OF JESUS, IT HAS BEEN LINKED WITH THE
TEMPLARS SINCE THE FOURTEENTH CENTURY.

RIGHT An oil painting
of the Holy Shroud from
the seventeenth century,
showing the fabric in
full, as it is held out by
an angel.

In 1357, the cloth made its first appearance on
record. Sightings of the image of a face on fabric
had been made previously, but it is not known
whether that was the same item. This cloth was
produced by the widow of the knight Geoffrey
de Charney, nephew of the Templar Geoffrey de
Charney who had died at the stake with De Molay

over 40 years previously. Madame de Charney put
the cloth on display in a church in Troyes, France.
Given the Templars' obsession with secrecy, if the
Shroud had been in their possession they might
have kept it hidden, but it is still not clear why it
was not used as one of their most revered relics. It
has been suggested that, during the Templars' trial,
the cloth had been smuggled away to the De
Charney family, who, after they thought a long

LEFT Detail of the face from the Turin Shroud,
which resides in Turin, Italy. The facial
impression is believed by many to be that of
Jesus Christ and the cloth to be the shroud
that covered his body after his death.

the date of the cloth as the sample they tested had been handled by many people over the centuries and was contaminated with bacteria. Since then, further scientific procedures have tried to resolve the issue, but they are all inconclusive. Some historians are convinced that the shroud is only about 700 years old, while others maintain that the system of stitching on the cloth establishes that it was from the first century.

A contradictory theory is that the Shroud is actually the image of Jacques de Molay. It is known that De Molay was tortured during his seven-year imprisonment. After the ordeal he was wrapped in a piece of cloth to soak up the blood, until he regained consciousness. If this is the case, then the Templars certainly did not worship the shroud, since it came to exist after the silencing of the Order.

LEFT A Christian worshipper lights candles at the site believed to be where Jesus Christ was crucified, in the Church of the Holy Sepulchre, Jerusalem. The church stands on the site of a temple dedicated to Aphrodite built during the Roman Empire. It was built by Constantine I in AD333, after he became Christian.

BELOW Entrance to the tomb of Christ, located in the Church of the Holy Sepulchre. During the Persian occupation of Jerusalem in AD614, most of the Church was ruined. When the Crusaders occupied Jerusalem in 1099, they built a new church, which still stands today.

eenough interval had passed, displayed it to raise money. In the Cluny Museum in Paris, the arms of De Charney and his widow can be seen on a pilgrim medallion, which also shows an image of the Shroud of Turin, indicating that it was in the family's possession for some time.

It has been suggested that the Templars obtained the relic in 1204 from the sack of Constantinople. It is unlikely that the Templars fought at Constantinople, but it is possible that they might have obtained this cloth as a gift.

SCIENTIFIC TESTING

Debates have raged over this piece of fabric. On the one hand, it has been dismissed as a forgery by many, including the bishop of Troyes when De Charney's widow first displayed it there. In 1978, a team tested the cloth with a variety of spectral imaging. They discovered that the image was imprinted, not painted, and that the dark red marks on the cloth are genuine bloodstains. They ascertained that the man died a traumatic and violent death, but they could not determine

MYSTERIOUS ICONOLATRY

THE IDEA THAT THE TEMPLARS WORSHIPPED A HEAD MANIFESTED ITSELF IN SEVERAL DIFFERENT WAYS, SOMETIMES LINKED WITH THE SKULL OF SIDON AND SOMETIMES WITH THE TURIN SHROUD. DURING THE TEMPLARS' SEVEN-YEAR IMPRISONMENT, THE INQUISITION OFTEN FOCUSED ON THE NOTION THAT THEY VENERATED AN IDOL NAMED BAPHOMET. ALTHOUGH IT IS SAID THAT SEVERAL TEMPLARS ADMITTED TO THIS (UNDER TORTURE OR THE THREAT OF TORTURE), THERE WAS NO INDICATION OF WHO OR WHAT BAPHOMET MIGHT HAVE BEEN, AS ALL THEIR CONFESSIONS WERE DIFFERENT. NO ONE SEEMS TO HAVE BEEN CLEAR ABOUT WHAT BAPHOMET REPRESENTED OR WHY IT HAD SPECIAL SIGNIFICANCE, AND ALL TEMPLARS RETRACTED THEIR CONFESSIONS LATER.

RIGHT Eliphas Lévi (1810–75), a French occult author and magician. drew his infamous impression of Baphomet which has had countless imitations. Statements had been obtained from arrested Knights Templar, stating that the Order secretly worshipped pagan idols, one of which was named as Baphomet. These confessions were obtained under torture and were later recanted.

It was believed by their accusers that Baphomet was an idol that the Templars worshipped in place of God. Some have inferred that the name "Baphomet" comes from "Mohammed", although Islam forbids all forms of idolatry. Baphomet was not the only idol that the Templars were accused of worshipping, but it was the principal one. Descriptions of it were diverse. Sometimes it was described as being a human skull, as having two faces, as being a cat- or goat-like creature or, alternatively, as a bearded or talking head.

RIGHT A stone carving of a royal head on a Templar church is one of many such carvings on Templar churches. Although these carvings were characteristic of the era, at the time of the Templars' downfall, they were thought to signify some of the Order's irregular practices.

The bearded head was mentioned often. Beards were not fashionable in the fourteenth century, but the Templars, as part of their Rule, wore beards. So perhaps the Inquisition was mocking them or implying that they were worshipping themselves. It is not known whether the head was a painting, carving or actual remains. At the time, it was thought that a severed human head aided certain forms of magic. In later legends, heads were said to have been worshipped by the Templars to enhance their wealth.

RELICS

During the Middle Ages, many devout Catholics placed great importance on physical items connected with saints, left from the time when the saint lived. It was believed that the saint was still physically present in objects that had once been connected with them. These could include clothes, possessions, objects that had been the cause of their death or actual bodily remains. These things were called relics, meaning "left behind". It was believed that the saint could act on Earth through their relics. The Templars venerated the relics in their keeping, as did all Holy Orders of the time.

MARTYRED HEADS

Alternatively, it has been suggested that this was the embalmed head of Jesus or of John the Baptist. Because St John the Baptist was beheaded, several versions of his head appeared regularly during the Middle Ages, each eventually disappearing into folklore. It was said that the Templars had this head as they were part of the Johannite heresy – which denounced Jesus as a false prophet and acknowledged John the Baptist

as the true Messiah. It is not clear why this suspicion arose, although in the course of their activities in the Holy Land, the Templars could have made contact with Johannite sects.

Since they were a Holy Order, relics were a part of the Templars' religious celebrations. They are known, for example, to have owned at least two heads of female martyrs. The first was St Euphemia, a female saint who had been martyred in AD303, which they kept in Cyprus after obtaining it from the sack of Constantinople. The second was possibly one of the 11,000 virgins martyred with St Ursula at Cologne, also at the beginning of the fourth century. These relics were often seen and openly acknowledged.

ABOVE *Martyrdom and Funeral of St Ursula*, 1493, by Carpaccio. The legend of St Ursula was popular during the Middle Ages. The power of relics in Christian devotion from the second to at least the sixteenth centuries was enormous and the Templars were proud to own them.

LEFT *The Apparition*, 1874–6 by G. Moreau shows the floating head of John the Baptist, regarded as a prophet by at least three religions, emblazoned by a magnificent halo, shocking Salome even though she requested it.

ENDURING SUPERSTITIONS

CURSES, SECRET COVENANTS AND THE POWER OF RELICS HAVE BEEN LINKED WITH THE TEMPLARS SINCE THEIR TRIALS. THE ENIGMAS OF THE CURSE OF JACQUES DE MOLAY, A MYSTERIOUS FLEET OF TEMPLAR SHIPS SAILING AWAY FROM FRANCE AND SECRET SYMBOLS CARVED IN PLACES ASSOCIATED WITH THE TEMPLARS HAVE INFLUENCED THESE STORIES. SOME ARE BASED ON HISTORICAL EVIDENCE, WHILE OTHERS SIMPLY DEMONSTRATE THE POWER OF SUPERSTITION. THE CURSE OF JACQUES DE MOLAY HAS PERPETUATED MYTHS OF TEMPLAR INVOLVEMENT WITH OCCULTISM. AS HE BURNED TO DEATH ON 18 MARCH 1314, DE MOLAY DECLARED HIS AND HIS ORDER'S INNOCENCE. HE SHOUTED: "ALL THOSE WHO HAVE ACTED AGAINST US WILL SUFFER FOR WHAT THEY HAVE DONE TO US".[7] POPE CLEMENT DIED JUST OVER A MONTH LATER, ALLEGEDLY FROM A SUDDEN ATTACK OF DYSENTERY AND PHILIP IV DIED IN A HUNTING ACCIDENT IN NOVEMBER OF THAT SAME YEAR.

RIGHT Early twentieth-century painting showing Richard the Lionheart surrendering to Saladin after the Battle of Hattin in 1187. The disastrous defeat seemed to herald a change in the fortunes of the Templars.

In 1314, Philip's real goal – to attain the Templars' wealth – had failed, as he never received their money. It is said that Templar treasure was taken away from the Paris Temple the night before the arrests – on 12 October 1307, secretly carried overland to the port of La Rochelle. A contemporary report states that 24 Templars boarded 18 galleys and the next day they had disappeared, never to be seen or heard

RIGHT The execution of King Louis XVI of France in January 1793. Some believe that the disposal of the French monarchy was the final retribution of Jacques de Molay and the Knights Templar, and there has been discussion to the effect that Templar descendants were revolutionaries themselves.

LEFT It is thought that
the Templars had a piece
of the True Cross: the
Cross upon which Jesus
was crucified, which they
revered as their most
holy relic. When they lost
it in the Battle of Hattin,
in 1187, it is said that
their rise to power
slowed down.

from again. Whether this is a true statement of
account or whether it is a false notion has never
been established.

DE MOLAY'S CURSE

The legend of De Molay's curse has been
embellished since his death. Chroniclers have
claimed that he cursed the entire line of
subsequent French kings as many died prematurely
and often horribly. Nearly 480 years later, on 21
January 1793, Louis XVI was led out to the
guillotine by revolutionaries. Moments after he
was executed, a man jumped on to the platform,
dipped his fingers into the king's blood and
shouted: "Jacques de Molay, you are avenged!"
The crowd cheered, all remembering the Templars
and believing that they had at last had their
revenge on the French monarchy.

HIDDEN WISDOM

On the exterior of Chartres Cathedral, by the
north door, there is a carving on a pillar
representing the Ark of the Covenant being
transported on a wheeled vehicle. Legend recounts
that the Ark of the Covenant was secreted deep
beneath the Temple in Jerusalem centuries before
the Templars arrived, that they found it and then
helped to finance the building of Chartres
Cathedral in order to hide the Ark beneath the
crypt. Similar legends claim that secret documents

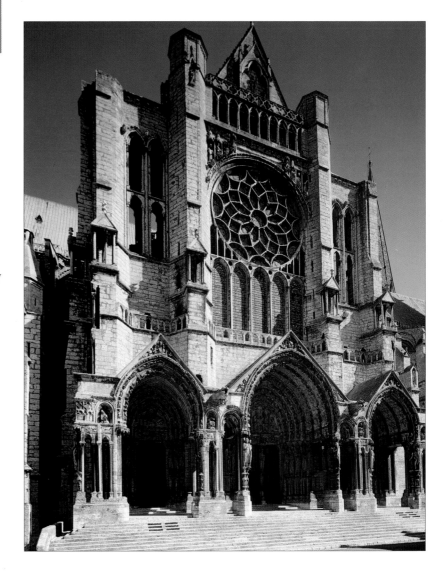

were also located beneath the Temple Mount.
There has been much speculation as to the exact
nature of these documents, but it is often claimed
that they contained scriptural scrolls, treatises on
sacred geometry and details of powerful, secret
knowledge, including art and science – hidden
wisdom of the ancient initiates of the Judaic and
Egyptian traditions.

ABOVE The north door
of Chartres Cathedral
in France, built in the
thirteenth century.
One of the Templar
legends surrounding
this cathedral is that
the Templars helped to
pay for its construction
in order to hide the Ark
of the Covenant inside.

TEMPLAR MYTHS

THE DRAMATIC RISE AND FALL OF ONE OF THE MOST POWERFUL INSTITUTIONS OF THE MEDIEVAL WORLD HAS FASCINATED PEOPLE FOR THE LAST SEVEN CENTURIES. THE TEMPLARS' TRIAL INEVITABLY COLOURS THE WAY WE VIEW THE KNIGHTS AND THE WAY THEY HAVE BEEN WRITTEN ABOUT. SOON AFTER THE ABOLITION OF THE ORDER, THERE WERE LEGENDS OF ESCAPED TEMPLARS, SECRET SOCIETIES, HIDDEN TREASURES, MYSTERIOUS SCROLLS, SECRETS AND CONNECTIONS WITH VARIOUS RELIGIONS.

BELOW Nineteenth-century drawing of *The Knights' March*, a poem by Alfred Lord Tennyson which perpetuated the romantic and idealized myths about medieval knights such as the Knights Templar.

It has been claimed that after the arrests, some escaped Templars hid in various tiny villages in the Alps. Folk tales from the period tell of "armed white knights" helping farmers to defeat Leopold of Austria. There are also records of Swiss villagers around that time suddenly becoming

skilled military negotiators. In the following years, the powerful Swiss banking system developed, shielded by secrecy and unlike any other banking system in the world. It is possible that the Templars' military and financial skills may have been the foundation of all of this.

ABOVE Westminster Abbey, which formerly contained the Stone of Scone in St Edward's Chair – upon which most English sovereigns have been crowned.

NOVEL IDEA

In 1819, Sir Walter Scott's *Ivanhoe* reinforced the idea that the Templars were arrogant and overbearing and the possessors of esoteric anti-Christian secrets. The novel was seized upon by composers, and between 1826 and 1891 seven operas appeared, using *Ivanhoe* as their storyline.

PRECIOUS STONE

Many of the Templar myths begin with the Order's occupation of the Temple platform in Jerusalem and their alleged excavations beneath it. The list of things that they found beneath it has been pored over and expanded upon. Yet, that site has little to do with Solomon. The base of the al-Aqsa mosque is early Roman and it is unlikely that anything could have been hidden there by earlier people without the Romans discovering it themselves.

The Stone of Scone (pronounced "scoon") might have been overlooked, however. The Stone, also known as the Stone of Destiny or Jacob's Pillow or Pillar Stone, is a block of sandstone believed to have been used by the biblical Jacob.

It was kept at the now ruined abbey in Scone, Scotland, and was used for centuries in the coronation of Scottish monarchs. In 1296 it was captured by Edward I and taken to Westminster Abbey where it was fitted into St Edward's Chair, upon which English sovereigns are crowned. However, it has been suggested that monks hid the real Stone, or that the Templars had the original Stone all along.

LINKS TO FREEMASONRY

Freemasonry emerged as a secret society towards the end of the seventeenth century. It is often claimed that Freemasonry was founded in Scotland in the early fourteenth century by Templars who escaped arrest. These claims were probably an effort to formalize the Freemasonry institution and give it an ancient lineage. Rosslyn Chapel was at the heart of Scottish Freemasonry. However, there is no historical evidence connecting the medieval Knights Templar to Freemasonry.

PLAYING CARDS

It has been said that the Templars invented playing or Tarot cards. According to this theory, in Tarot cards, the fool represents the novice of the Order and the hanged man a Knight, but there is no evidence for this, or any explanation as to why the Templars would have created the cards.

ABOVE A junior warden introduces a candidate to a Lodge for admission as an apprentice Freemason in the seventeenth century.

ABOVE LEFT Edward I's Coronation Chair, which contained the Stone of Scone. Kenneth McAlpin, the first king of the Scots and the Picts, is said to have brought the Stone to Scone in AD843. Edward I captured the sacred Stone from the Scots and had an oak chair made for it. The lions are a recent addition, likely from the Tudor period.

ABOVE The Knight, a sixteenth-century Tarot card designed by Antonio Cicognara.

TEMPLAR LEGACY

BY ABOUT 1300, THE TEMPLARS HAD BUILT A NETWORK OF AT LEAST 870 CASTLES, PRECEPTORIES AND SUBSIDIARIES OF HOUSES. SEVERAL EXAMPLES OF THESE CAN BE FOUND IN VARIOUS COUNTRIES THROUGHOUT WESTERN EUROPE. MOST OF THESE WERE TAKEN OVER BY THE HOSPITALLERS AFTER THE TEMPLARS' DEMISE. ONCE THE POPE ANNOUNCED THE ABOLITION OF THE ORDER IN 1312, HE INSISTED THAT ALL TEMPLAR LANDS AND POSSESSIONS WERE HANDED OVER TO THE HOSPITALLERS, MUCH TO THE FURY OF PHILIP IV. THE KING IMMEDIATELY SUED THE HOSPITALLERS FOR THE LEGAL COSTS OF THE TRIAL. MANY HOSPITALLERS HAD TO WAIT TILL WELL AFTER 1314 TO TAKE OVER THE TEMPLAR PROPERTIES, AS PHILIP AND OTHER EUROPEAN MONARCHS TRIED TO HOLD ON TO THEM.

ABOVE This Knights Templar castle at Ponferrada, Spain, was built along a sacred route where pilgrims have traditionally travelled to the tomb of St James.

philosophy. They pushed new medical ideas forward, by becoming adept in the use of drugs, and producing their own physicians and surgeons. Their hospitals and infirmaries were forerunners of modern hospitals, and long before anyone else considered it necessary, they promoted the importance of hygiene. Their use of the Atbash cipher for coded communication is an idea that has since been used regularly in warfare. This means the tangible legacies are every bit as powerful as their more indefinable ones.

The Templar legacy lives on. Much of what we do today in banking, trading, communications, farming and shipping owe something to the innovations of the Order of the Poor Knights of the Temple of Solomon. Among other things, their pioneering international banking schemes introduced the cheque and credit systems. They contributed to improvements in surveying, cartography, road building and navigation and were among the first Europeans to use a magnetic compass.

From the relationships they established with other cultures in the East, the Templars gained advancements in science, architecture and

RIGHT The Templars' Rotunda of the Convent of Christ in Tomar, Portugal; a stronghold built in 1160 by Gualdim Pais, the provincial Master there.

LEFT The Church of the Holy Sepulchre in Cambridge is usually called the Round Church and was built by the Knights Templar in 1130. It was meant to emulate the Church of the Holy Sepulchre in Jerusalem and is one of only four surviving round medieval churches in Britain. The small nave is encircled by large Norman pillars, though the conical roof was added in the nineteenth century.

ABOVE The red cross of St George was used to signify a "Soldier of Christ" to the Crusaders. St George was the patron saint of many Crusaders and the Templars wore the red cross on their left breast. Both the French and the English, who fought with the Templars, first wore St George's cross in the twelfth century.

ENDURING REPRESENTATION

Many symbols associated with the Templars have evolved into modern usage. The flag of England is the red St George's Cross on a white background. St George was styled as the Crusader Saint and his red cross is the cross of the Templars. The Red Cross has been passed down as an international symbol of healing and medicine.

THE CHINON PARCHMENT

In 1312, Pope Clement V announced the abolition of the Order. Yet a parchment was found in 2002 by Dr Barbara Frale in the Vatican archives that proves that Clement made sure that his own representatives questioned De Molay and other leading Templars in the dungeons of Chinon castle in the Loire in 1308. The Chinon Parchment is a long-lost document that indicates that the Pope secretly absolved Jacques de Molay and the rest of the Templars in 1308 from the charges brought against them.

Noting that De Molay and the other Templars had asked his pardon, the Pope wrote: "We hereby decree that they are absolved by the Church and may again receive Christian sacraments". This amounted to the complete exoneration of the Order, but the Pope did not make this absolution public because the scandal of the Templars had

aroused extreme passions and he feared a church schism. Philip IV had De Molay and other Templar leaders put to death before the Pope's verdict could be published, and it was subsequently lost.

Perhaps, in the end, the most enduring legacy of the Templars is the fascination they continue to exert over us. It might be that the whole truth about them will never be fully understood, but intrigue and mysteries will continue to abound about the first military monks.

LEFT The Atbash Cipher is a simple substitution cipher where the first letter of the alphabet is exchanged with the last letter of the alphabet and so on. The Enigma machine shown here was more complex than the Atbash cipher, but was based on similar principles and was used for secret messaging during World War II.

Glossary

Apprentice's Pillar
Also known as the Prentice Pillar; this is a decorated column in the fifteenth-century Rosslyn Chapel in Scotland. The pillar gets its name from a legend involving the mason in charge of the stonework in the chapel and his young apprentice. According to the legend, the mason did not believe he could carve the column without seeing the original that formed the inspiration for the design, in Rome. On his return the apprentice had completed the column and in a fit of jealous rage, the mason killed the apprentice.

Apse
A large semicircular or polygonal recess, arched or with a domed roof, usually at the eastern end of a church.

Ark of the Covenant
Sacred wooden chest where the ancient Hebrews kept the two tablets containing the Ten Commandments.

Assassins
An order founded in Persia and Syria during the eleventh century, and a development of the Shiite division of Islam. They encouraged mathematics and philosophy, and are said to have used hashish as a means of obtaining celestial visions. They are famous for their murderousness, especially during the Crusades.

Atbash
A simple substitution cipher which consists of substituting the first letter of the alphabet for the last, the second for the one before last, and so on, reversing the alphabet.

Baphomet
A strange idol or image of uncertain origin, sometimes believed to be a demon.

Byzantine
A citizen of the Byzantine Empire, or a native Greek during the Middle Ages.

Casal
A Templar Knight commander of knights, houses and farms and responsible for the daily business of various estates under his care.

Cathars
A Christian dualist sect in southern France during the twelfth and thirteenth centuries, also known as Albigensians.

Chapter
The local branch of a brotherhood of the Knights Templar.

Cistercians
A Roman Catholic order of enclosed monks, also known as White Monks (from the colour of their habit, over which is worn a black scapular or apron).

Commandery
Another term for preceptory.

Consecrated
Declared sacred in Christian belief.

Crusade
Series of military campaigns – usually sanctioned by the Pope – that took place during the eleventh to thirteenth centuries. Originally, they were Christian attempts to re-capture the Holy Land from the Muslims, but some were directed against other Europeans, such as the Fourth Crusade against Constantinople, the Albigensian Crusade against the Cathars of southern France and the Northern Crusades.

Franks
A Germanic tribe which conquered most of Gaul and eventually established a powerful state centred in what is modern France and Germany, but whose borders extended well beyond.

Infidel
Unbelievers or people who do not believe in a particular religion.

Knights Hospitallers
Members of the military and religious Benedictine Order of St John of Jerusalem. The symbol of the Order came to be a white cross worn on a black robe.

Mamluks
Slave soldiers used by Muslim caliphs and the Ottoman Empire, who often seized power for themselves and who overthrew the Christians in the Holy Land.

Mongols
A number of Inner Asian tribes that were united by Genghis Khan in 1206.

Nave
The nave is the central approach to the high altar, from the Medieval Latin *navis*, "ship".

Necromancy
The practice of supposedly communicating with the spirits of the dead in order to predict the future.

Nova Scotia
(*Nouvelle-Écosse* in French) A Canadian province located on Canada's southeastern coast. Its name is Latin for New Scotland.

Outremer
French for "overseas", the general name given to the Crusader states established after the First Crusade, especially the Kingdom of Jerusalem.

Palfrey
A light horse used for ordinary riding.

Papal bull
A special kind of charter issued by the Pope and named after the seal (*bulla*) that was attached to the end to authenticate it.

Preceptory
Monastic house of the Order of the Templars.

Relic
An object, especially a piece of the body or a personal item of someone of religious significance, carefully preserved with an air of veneration as a tangible memorial.

Romanesque
Architectural style prevalent in Europe *c.* AD900 –1200, with massive vaulting and round arches.

Sacred geometry
Geometry used in the design of sacred architecture or art. The belief is that geometry and mathematical ratios are also the basis of music, cosmology and other features of the natural universe. This belief was held in ancient and medieval times and influenced the construction of temples and churches and the creation of religious art.

Sangreal
Another term for Holy Grail, the cup that Jesus drank from at the last supper. In Old French, *san graal* or *san grial* means "Holy Grail" and *sang rial* means "royal blood".

Seneschal
Deputy to the Grand Master of the Order of the Temple.

Sepulchre
A burial vault or cave, or a tomb made of rock, stone or brick.

Sidon
The third largest city in Lebanon, 48 km (30 miles) from Beirut. Its name means "a fishery". After the First Crusade, it became a chief property in the Kingdom of Jerusalem.

Skull and crossbones
A traditional symbol, used on Templar gravestones, of two crossed femurs (thigh bones) topped by a skull, indicating bodily remains.

Teutonic Order
German crusading military order under Roman Catholic religious vows, formed at the end of the twelfth century in Acre to give medical aid to pilgrims.

True Cross
The wooden cross upon which Jesus was crucified.

Turcopoles
Light cavalry, part of the Order of the Templars, usually of Arab descent.

Vernacular
Materials, styles and techniques native to the builders.

Vizier
High-ranking Islamic minister or adviser.

Votus
A vow sworn by Crusaders, to be fulfilled on successfully reaching Jerusalem, where they were granted a cloth cross to be sewn into their clothes. It comes from the Latin *votus* meaning "vowed" or "desired". The original meaning is preserved in the word "devoted".

INDEX

BIBLIOGRAPHY

The many books and articles written on the Knights Templar are daunting. There is so much research and so many viewpoints and opinions on the topic that it can be confusing to know what to read and what to believe. Most books on the subject fall into two camps: the academic and the more speculative. Some are simply seeking sensationalism, while others are serious academic studies. The Internet similarly has a mix of helpful and edifying information on some sites, with fantastic or incredible ideas that should not be taken seriously on others. Here are some of the books offering many theories and perspectives that are worth reading:

Baigent, Michael; Leigh, Richard and Lincoln, Henry
The Holy Blood and The Holy Grail (Arrow, 1996)

Barber, Malcolm
The New Knighthood, A History of the Order of the Temple (Cambridge University Press, 1994)

Burman, Edward
Supremely Abominable Crimes, The Trial of the Knights Templar (Allison & Busby, 1994)

Cantor, Norman F. (ed.)
The Pimlico Encyclopedia of the Middle Ages (Pimlico, 1999)

Collins, Roger
Early Medieval Europe, 300-1000 (London, 1991)

Demurger, Alain
The Last Templar (Profile Books, 2002)

Forey, Alan J.
The Military Orders from the Twelfth to the Early Fourteenth Centuries (Basingstoke Macmillan, 1991)

Howarth, Stephen
The Knights Templar (London, 1982)

Laidler, Keith
The Head of God; the Lost Treasure of the Templars (London, 1998)

Lord, Evelyn
The Knights Templar in Britain (Pearson Education Ltd, 2004)

Maalouf, Amin (translated by John Rothschild)
The Crusades through Arab Eyes (London, 1984)

Martin, Sean
The Knights Templar, The History and Myths of the Legendary Military Order (Thunder's Mouth Press, 2005)

Nelson, Janet L. (ed.)
Richard Coeur de Lion in History and Myth (London, 1992)

Nicholson, Helen
The Knights Templar a New History (Sutton Publishing, 2001)

Nicholson, Helen
Templars, Hospitallers and Teutonic Knights, Images of the Military Orders, 1128-1291 (Leicester, 1993)

Partner, Peter
The Murdered Magicians (Oxford University Press, 1981)

Read, Piers Paul
The Templars (Weidenfeld & Nicholson, 1999)

Riley-Smith, Jonathan (ed.)
The Oxford Illustrated History of the Crusades (Oxford, 1995)

Seward, Desmond
The Monks of War: the Military Religious Orders (Penguin Books, 1992)

Sinclair, Andrew
The Sword and the Grail (Century, 1993)

Footnotes
[1] Quoted in Oliver J Thatcher and Edgar Holmes McNeal, eds, *A Source book for Medieval History.*
[2] Quoted in Helen Nicholson, "Saints or Sinners? The Knights Templar in medieval Europe." *History Today (1994)*, pp. 30-37.
[3] Quoted in Barber, *The New Knighthood, A History of the Order of the Temple*, p. 16.
[4] Quoted in Read, *The Templars*, p. 277.
[5] Quoted in Sean Martin, *The Knights Templar the History and Myths of the Legendary Military Order*, p. 138.
[6] Quoted in Michael Baigent, Richard Leigh & Henry Lincoln, *Holy Blood, Holy Grail*, p. 81.
[7] Quoted in Helen Nicholson, *The Knights Templar a New History*, p. 223.